Art Is

Art Is

A Journey into the Light

Makoto Fujimura

YALE UNIVERSITY PRESS   NEW HAVEN & LONDON

Yale University Press books may be purchased in quantity for
educational, business, or promotional use. For information, please email
sales.press@yale.edu (U.S. office) or sales@yaleup.co.uk (U.K. office).

Designed by Dustin Kilgore.
Set in Ivy Ora Type by Motto Publishing Services.
Printed in Czechia.

Library of Congress Control Number: 2025930820
ISBN 978-0-300-27365-6 (hardcover)

A catalogue record for this book is available from the British Library.

Authorized Representative in the EU: Easy Access System Europe,
Mustamäe tee 50, 10621 Tallinn, Estonia, gpsr.requests@easproject.com

10 9 8 7 6 5 4 3 2 1

Contents

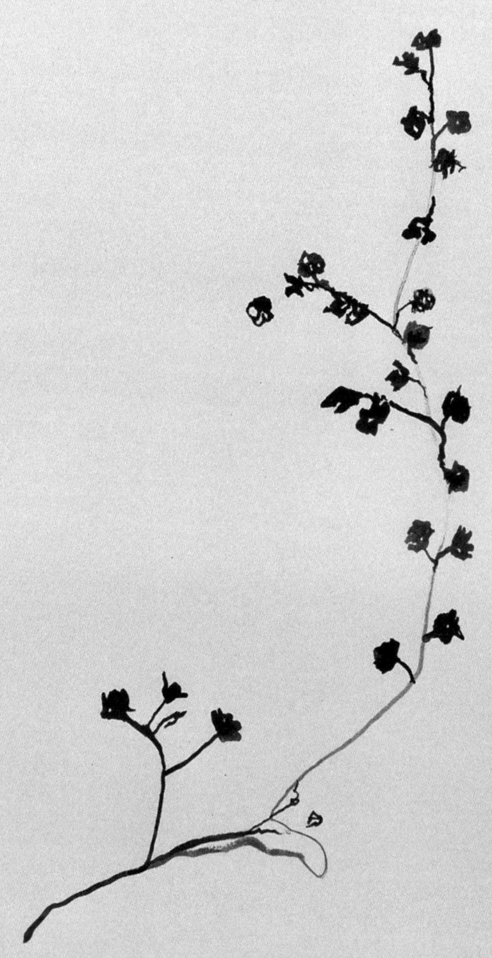

Chapter 1

Thresholds

To see a World in a Grain of Sand
And a Heaven in a Wild Flower
Hold Infinity in the palm of your hand
And Eternity in an hour
—William Blake, *Auguries of Innocence*, 1803

My studio, a converted horse barn, awaits me as I stroll through a row of lanky Armstrong maples, on a flat stone path, a gentle curve around the iris and peony beds.

A mason bee box hangs on a worn post by the barn door. Little bamboo tubes, stacked-up pipes inside their little wooden box, are capped with mud in wintertime, allowing the solitary bees to have their "capsule hotel" home. They are the first bees to come out after the cold, wiggling their dark fuzzy bottoms out first, exposed to the chill of the morning air. In the summer, bee balms, planted behind the peonies intentionally to contrast their purple haze against the red barn, invite the mason bees, the honeybees, and the fat bumblebees roaming about in search of beauty. Coreopsis dance below the tall bee balms, with their vermillion and gold

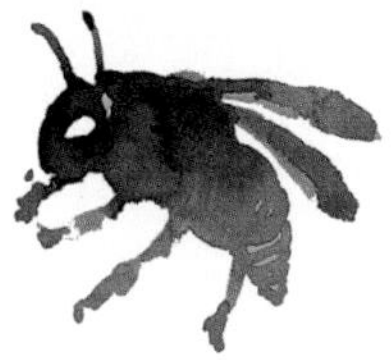

"Mason Bee" illustration, watercolor and sumi ink
on paper. Copyright © 2024 Makoto Fujimura.

crowns cast in the shifting wind. In a bright May morning, the tree swallows will arrive after a three-thousand-mile trek from the south of Mexico, in their handsome iridescent dark green—the same color as my heated malachite—arcing the cerulean sky. They swish above the uncut grassy areas, moving slightly the tips of the blades every time.

Awareness

"What is art?" Throughout this book, I implicitly ask this question with markers for our journey into the light. Rather than giving tidy definitions, I ask generative questions. The title of this book is "Art

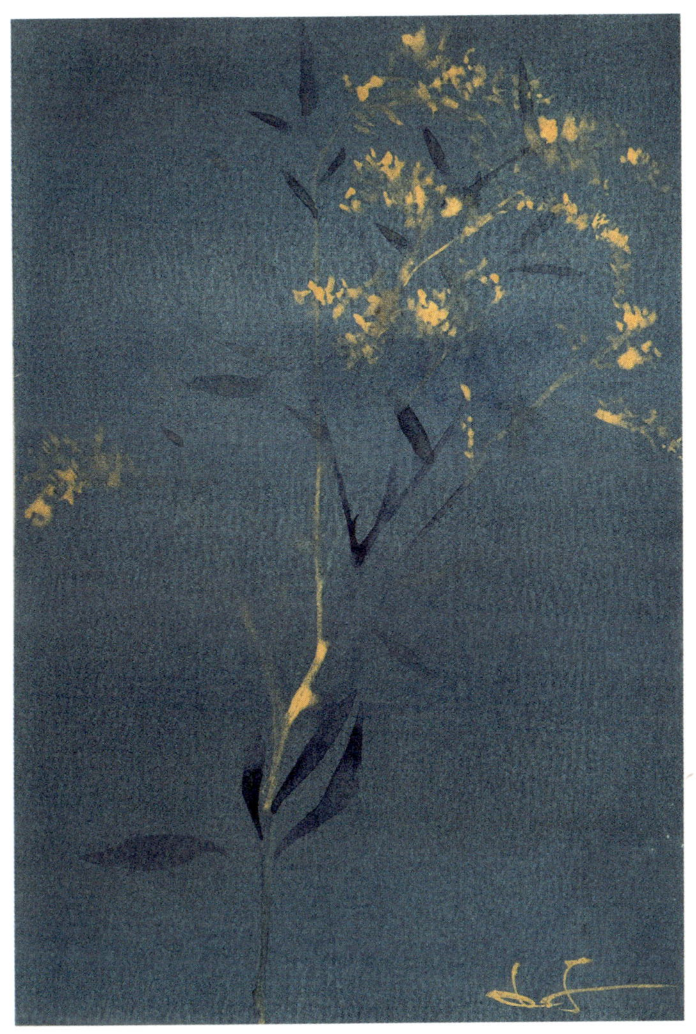

Goldenrod, 2024, mineral pigments and gold on paper.
Copyright © 2024 Makoto Fujimura.

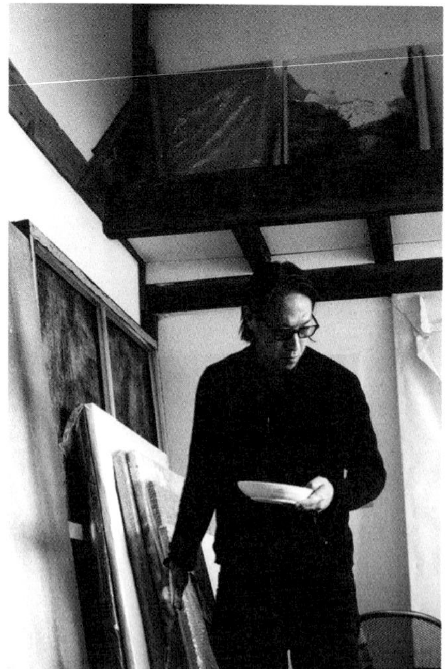

Makoto Fujimura in the studio.
Photo credit Alyson LeCroy.

Is," and that statement may not be so much a question as a revelation about how "Art Exists" in my paintings. Art exists here, in my studio, as open-ended quest-ions to ponder. Art is the quest of what "Life is." Art reveals both life and death, toward generative hopes and destructive ends.

Art is awareness. Art is being made aware of our world, full of wonderment and sorrows. Art is an expression beyond "self-expression," a path toward uncovering beauty in complexity, mysteries, and even the darkness of the unknown. Art that is trapped in hedonism or narcissism will not endure, and worse yet, can become an unwitting (or witting) agent for destruction. Surely, art can also capture our darkness, and art can expose what is hidden. Art can, simultaneously, be the stench of death in the soil as well as the pungent aroma of spring narcissus. But the challenge for artists is to be aware in that complex process of creativity, so by emptying our egos we honestly make ourselves fully present in the world. We need to pay attention so as not to participate in the sinister works of the darkness, often arising from our heart's malaise. In a world in which we have created division, destruction, death, and culture war schism, art witnesses what our eyes already know—the prismatic light invades and pushes aside our preconceived categories and gently opens our hearts to see grace permeating the universe.

An artist sees in a panoramic mode, seeing through a wider lens. At the same time, artists also take note of the "Minute Particulars" of their worlds, as William Blake puts it, and every detail, from mason bees to coreopsis, can become a generative entry point toward the expansive world.[1] Grace (*charis* in Greek, as Saint Paul writes) enters through our senses: it is what we cannot recognize, what cannot be marketed and therefore easily distorted and traded; art is ultimately a gift, as grace is a gift.

AS I WALK TO THE STUDIO, the *Amsonias*, or bluestars, greet me as well. In the spring, white azurite flowers look like stars, spreading out their gentle tails, and the morning dew prisms the sunrise, oblique lights gently caressing the feathery bushes. In the details of their design, I begin to sketch, in my mind, on a vast horizontal canvas, with gold *sunago* spread over dark azurite blue. Sunago (literally "sand children") is a Japanese *Nihonga* technique of forcing the gold leaf to be broken into fragments through a grid. Just as I am pondering how the sunago gold will cascade into the crevices of the buckling paper, I notice the creeping thyme invading the cracks between the stones, thus making itself vulnerable to my footsteps. Thyme grows when it is stepped on, with whiskers probing into the stone, so my gentle intrusion is most welcome, as its faint aroma of resilience prepares me to paint. Speedwells scatter their violet colors, specks of delight even in the early morning frost. I am drawn toward that faint light of insight and delight that awaits me in the studio. Thus, by the time I enter the studio, I have already painted many paintings in my mind. In Japanese tradition, nature *becomes* culture, and Japanese art is deeply connected to nature: the complexities and beauty of natural realms are honed and honored in art.

I think of Sen no Rikyū, the great tea master of sixteenth-century Japan, who created the Japanese tea ceremony (*sado* or *chanoyu*) as a practice of awareness, a ritual of peacemaking resistance to dictatorial powers during feudal times of war. Rikyū was very intentional in communicating without words, through subtle but complex gestures, carefully but simply, as placing a fallen maple leaf glistening in the morning dew on a moss-covered stone to suggest a path to peace, and even a type of repentance. He models for us how our lives can

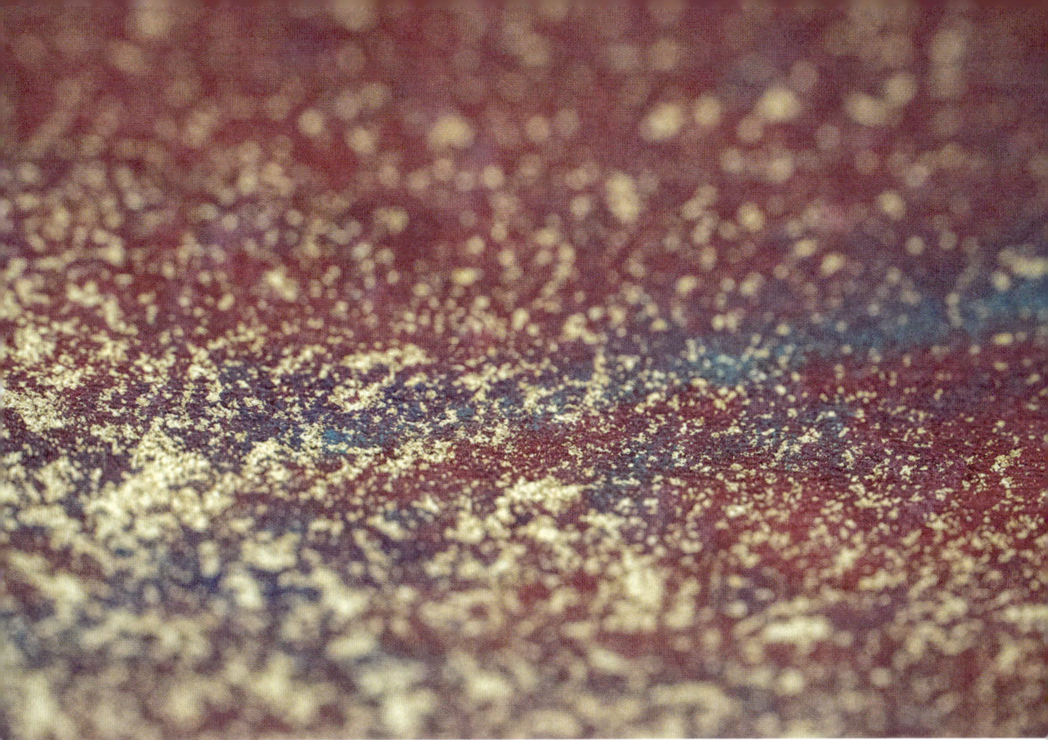

Lux Aeterna (detail), 2021, mineral pigments, gold, and gesso on canvas. Copyright © 2021 Makoto Fujimura. Photo credit Hazel Thompson, 2024.

be an artful peacemaking in violent times. He is a primary example of how we may inject *charis* into our fragmented, conflicted world.

Science and Research

I was born in Boston when my father was doing postdoctoral work in linguistics research with Noam Chomsky, who is known for generative grammar theory.[2] My father developed his own thesis to introduce generative grammar theory to Japan. We then went to Sweden for my father's research stint, then to Tokyo University. We lived in Kamakura, Japan, a twelfth- to fourteenth-century historic capital. It was there where I spent my early schooling years and where my aesthetics were formed. Later, my father was recruited by Bell Labs in Murray Hill, New Jersey, as a speech and hearing scientist. I grew up to be an artist in an environment full of scientists, always having to navigate cultures foreign to me, immersed in a language that I still struggle to master.

Even as a college student in the United States, I felt like an "outsider" looking in on an alien culture; if you ask me today where "home" is, I will say that I am most comfortable not fitting in. Just like the tree swallows, I've traveled far, knowing that my "home" may always be nomadic. Since I've struggled with languages all my life, I found art to be my primary way of communicating.

This book, perhaps, is a result of years of trying to communicate the impossible, to "walk on water" as I draw out the path to the light.[3] I have always considered art to be impossible. How can I create beauty, describe the wonderments of what I see, when my own heart is darkened, broken, and shattered? How can I create beauty in a world full of violence and death? What I see are often glimpses, fragmented sketches rather than perfected, complete paintings. What if, I nevertheless consider, the line I draw can lead the reader into the heart's meandering paths, even hardened hearts of stone? What if the unknown, the mystery of our lost journey is reawakened by being aware, in between knowing and not knowing.

Many of the materials I use, as I describe in detail in this book, were used in sixteenth-century Japan, methods now commonly known as Nihonga, of pulverized minerals, such as azurite and malachite, mixed in hide glue. The pigments are prismatic, refracting lights of microscopic rainbow hues, especially when they are layered over time. My art, therefore, is "slow art," requiring more than a hundred layers before I start to paint any movement or images, and then the surface will sometime rest over years before the images reveal themselves.

Nest-Making for Peace

We can see a bluebird box from our north-facing kitchen windows in front of the old Asian pear tree. White malachite lichens cover the jagged branches. This aged tree was planted a long time ago by a farmer on the top of the hill. Before that farmer settled here, these plateau hills belonged to the indigenous Lenape tribe, native stewards who fished for shad in the streams beyond the pear tree.

Perhaps the bluebirds inherited the animosity bled into this land, land on which George Washington's troops might have trod, a land worth fighting over. I have learned in caring for the land that bluebirds are highly territorial and will spend the entire nesting season fighting away the swallows, chickadees, and wrens. The azurite males become obsessed, too busy fighting to nest, I've found, with only one box installed. Peace is created immediately, however, if I place two other bluebird boxes about six feet apart. Other birds will then be allowed to nest in the outer boxes, which provide a cease-fire agreement. I peeked into the bluebird nest box once out of curios-

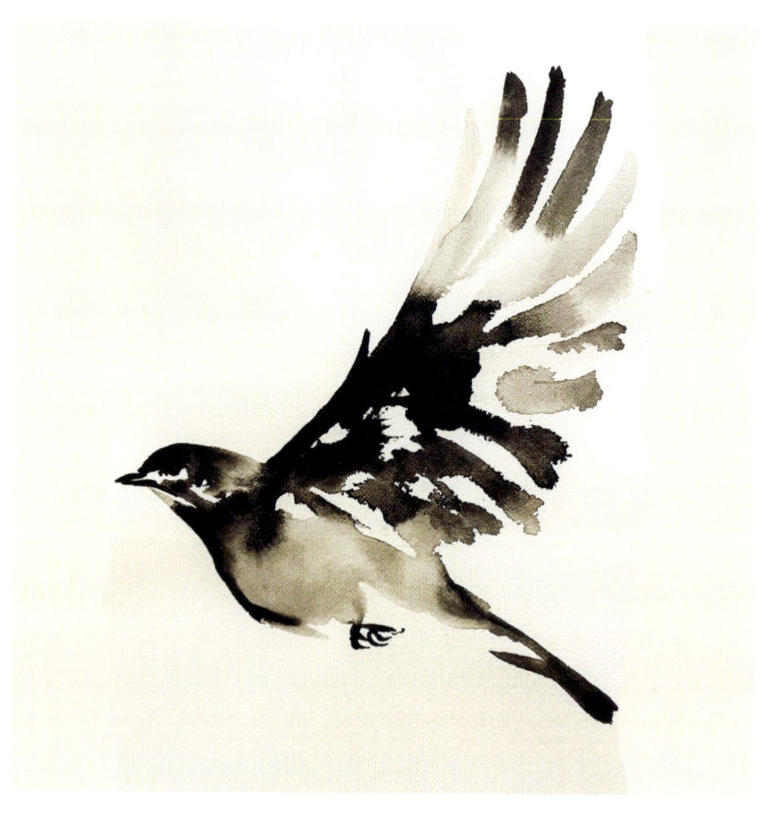

"Bluebird" detail, sumi ink on paper.
Copyright © 2024 Makoto Fujimura.

ity; in the crevice, with the precision of their sharp, thin beaks, they had built a nest of pine needles formed with fragile, soft weavings, a cushion of belonging and nurture. In it were three white azurite eggs.

My art making, likewise, begins by creating a crevice, a sliver of peacemaking, suited for my highly introverted nature. I get to create a delicate home through my art for nomadic souls to rest. What I write from that fragile nest flows out into an already graced, sacred process of art making, a journey perhaps as ancient as three magi following the patterns of signs in the stars.

I have followed such a path of discovery through the desert of life, often not knowing what I will find at the end of the journey. Just like the magi being invited into King Herod's quarters, I have been invited to today's version of "the king's private quarters" along the way, finding myself in such places as the inner corridors of the White House or speaking to members of Parliament in a banquet hall overlooking the Thames River, but I have also been "warned in a dream" by my conscience to not follow the patterns of power.[4] I instead follow the stars to a vulnerable babe in a manger. I marvel now that such a lonely path has led to an oasis of abundance; that babe in the manger turned out to be quite a miracle worker.

In college, I struggled to write just one paragraph of English, being in between cultures and languages. I have continued to write, as I watch my paint dry, relying on my cultural heritage to integrate writing and painting. Japanese writings are often lyrical and allusive, rather than linear and descriptive. They are image-based and focus on the affective and do not have clear outlines of an argument. I had to find my own path of making, and in my case, my writings began to flow out of such meandering markers of creating my paintings. Writing, such as this book, has become essential for the process of making my paintings, with my writing becoming part of my discipline of attentiveness. The slow evaporation of the paint, like an invisible tide of words, rises upon these pages, hovering over the many layers.

The studio spaces became a refuge as a quiet place of making. During my student days, there was no way that anyone could get me to stand up in front of a crowd to speak, even in my native tongue. After my "inversion" into faith (see "Behind the Veil," Section 1, below), I began to sense an unction to stand in the gap between my sacred space of creativity and the world. I realized as I began to speak about my works that I can follow the patterns of the stars, and report to a cynical world of what I have seen, a miracle in a manger. By doing so, that process of discovery invites the audience into my own creative process, and my studio. Everything, therefore, flows out of my studio where I see the miraculous every day. My journey has been a journey of impossibilities.[5]

New Paths

Back in the '90s, it was taboo to have an artist talk event in the art world of New York City. Speaking about one's own work was a sign of weakness, for artists should never talk about their work, as if it needs explanation. I transgressed this implicit rule and pushed against my own introverted nature, in New York galleries during the

'90s, becoming one of the first visual artists to have an artist talk event at an exhibit.

I spoke of my Nihonga materials and Isaiah 61 (an "inauguration" poem that Jesus began his ministry with). Apparently, I possess a contrarian nature along with my shyness; anything that was taboo to do, I thought worth trying. Artists were not supposed to speak of beauty in those days, as beauty at the time was seen as suspect in the "serious" ideation of contemporary art. Beauty was the remains of the imperialistic past. I introduced terms such as Nihonga, and, more recently, *Kintsugi*, to these cynical audiences. I defined "beauty" not in Western terms only but based on my deeper root of beauty in Japanese culture.

Such a "migratory" journey led me into the gaps—the gaps of normative categories of cultures, art, and even theology, even though in all these realms, I am orthodox, perhaps in stubbornness, in practice, and in my thinking. I am weaving the ancient patterns of nest-making, repeating the liturgy of beauty, and paying attention to the remnants. The making journey dwells in the gaps left behind by the prevalent false binaries of culture wars; oppositions of politics, race, and the "we-versus-them" mentality; flashy celebrity creations of "influencers" that drive the market and define our culture today. We place easy labels upon each other, and market and political forces use those labels to divide us. Culture war memes are easily manipulated by the algorithms of social media. The labels diminish us and make us fight territorial battles.

I sometimes imagine the Lenape fishers catching shad, refracting in the air in one of the streams that surround us. Our journey into the light is a prismatic journey toward a spectrum of generative and abundant possibilities, but our present powers, languages, and structures do not allow us to have a language to dream with, as dreams are made of fragile and impossible hopes. We are too fragmented and polarized, our soils too tainted with the poison of culture wars to grow lasting cultural crops, or to even envision a common march toward the Promised Land of plenty. Art is for all peoples marching toward that Promised Land of abundance yet faced with the severe scarcity of our "Wasteland" ashes.

"Thus we cover the universe," says Gaston Bachelard, "with drawings we have lived."[6] My journey into the studio every day is part of that drawing, following the trace of line that began long ago when I was a child. Then, later, it became a "scribble in the sand" (John 8:11) on Ground Zero ashes, a line that seems to disappear into darkness and trauma, but a line that desperately seeks the light, a line that weaves together art, faith, and ultimately the love that binds together the universe. In short, I have set up my life so that I can create into the gaps and in-between spaces where machine algorithms of culture wars cannot reach, because there is always a "ghost in the machine" (in my case, a beautiful ghost),[7] or an unintended outcome of reductive tasks. My lines are also pulverized and refractive, appearing and disappearing into these pages.

Such a journey may be seen as an act of resistance against the status quo; but like the solitary mason bees, I take flight faithfully every day, meandering in between cultures and languages, to discern and

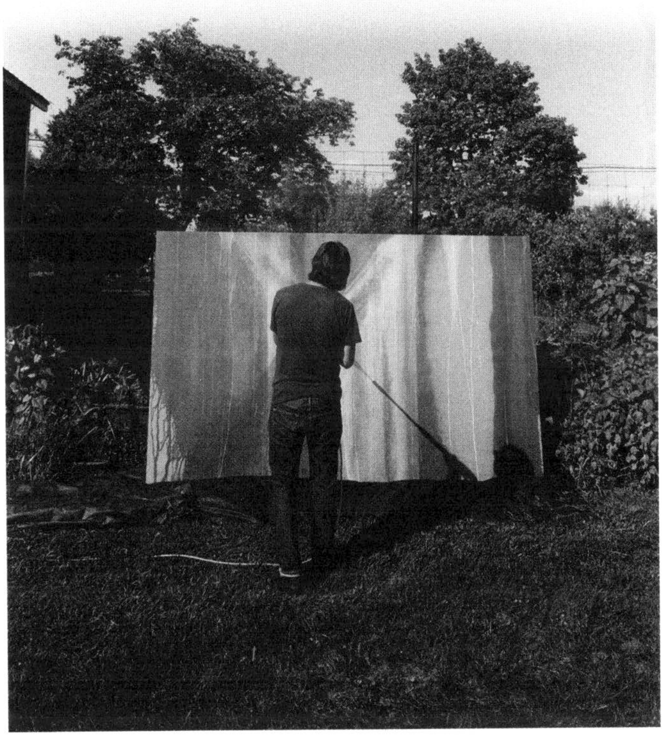

Makoto Fujimura painting outdoors.
Photo credit Alyson LeCroy.

find true and real flowers. Art in that sense has always been a quest for authenticity. Mason bees have a purpose: to find flowers to pollinate, and yet, they meander.[8] Art meanders to inaugurate the new. Writing, too, is an introspective journey with vulnerable footsteps of a soul's pilgrimage toward the truth. The process of writing, like layers of painting, seeks to create a refractive experience with words as prismatic shards of our spiritual journey toward the light.

A Spiritual Quest

A major art critic once told me kindly that if I did not associate myself with Christianity, I would be known as one of the great sublime painters of our time. I thanked him for this greatest compliment. But for me, I am not associating myself with the institution of what is known as "Christianity"—I am a follower of Jesus, whom I found by following the stars. I follow Jesus, the greatest artist.[9] I am drawing out what it means to live out that faith to make beauty, to serve to create communities of abundance along the way (see "Behind the Veil," below). Many assume that Christianity is a "Western religion" and find strange my association of "slow art," of the "Eastern" technique of Nihonga, with the church. I tell them that the Bible is an Eastern document, originating in the Middle *East,* then affecting the refinement of Western civilization and giving birth to occidental sciences. The content of the Hebrew scriptures, of what Christians call the "Old Testament," culturally is better understood in Asian cultures (for example, reading the book of Jeremiah or Lamentations in Japanese has a deeper resonance), rather than in our language of

American individualism. Many Christian mystics throughout history (from Saint Teresa to Thomas Merton) have had ascetic values closer to those of Zen Buddhism than to Western industrialism, even as these mystics sought their spiritual center in the historic figure of Jesus.

In between the cracks created by the incessant culture wars, East verses West, and market categories, I found a meaningful place to nest. I have called this journey a "culture care" path.[10] Culture care is to steward the soil of culture, as gardeners tend to their gardens. Just as the gaps of stone steps leading to my studio allow speedwell flowers to thrive, the gaps resulting from years of culture wars can invite unique beauty. My meandering journey between East and West can also open our eyes toward a language of peace that transcends these barriers. Markets demand identifiable brands, using "Christian" as a label and as an adjective, but my faith is a noun and a verb that points to a renewal of all brokenness and loss. Even in our polarized times, full of pulverized fragments, I am determined to continue to care for my land and learn from the soil how to steward our culture well, and my slow art flows out of that care.

Perhaps not obvious to many, but clearly evident to me, is that this integration of art and faith was not anticipated but only given as a gift of grace, *charis*. Such an integration, and improvisation, is unfortunately rare in the art world and in the church, both with power bases that function as if the system knows that we are to be easily manipulated. My journey as an artist proves that there are other paths. We all have a "homing compass" inside of us to map out our paths, again, just like the mason bees coming out in early spring to look for the first blossoms after a long winter. If we can cultivate our journey toward the light, by relying on what is already inside of us, what the Quakers called the "the Inner Light," we may find where the beauty resides. Yet, as I've continually confronted in my own self, there is yet darkness that we cannot see.[11]

Art requires that we be vulnerable to the darkness as well as to the light. I have been taught that there is a difference between depicting the darkness and participating in the darkness.[12] Depicting darkness is the *Guernica* of Picasso, an elegy to the atrocity of war, and such an act of "transgression" against atrocities is necessary. But at any point, the darkness we cannot see can misguide and confuse our journey toward the light. As artists, even in pushing back against injustice, we can end up participating in evil by joining the violence and the blame shifting, rather than practicing the art of nonviolent resistance, as well as the generational hard work of truth-telling and the ultimately hopeful work of uncovering evil into the light. Such blind spots need to be examined through our art, and our lives as well. Art is a path to honestly grapple with all that is within and without. There is a Greek word, *metanoia,* which is translated "repentance." Repentance is "re-pentence," which is to re-consider our journeys.

Re-pentence

Metanoia literally means to turn 180 degrees around. I am a survivor of September 11, 2001, having spent forty-five harrowing minutes trapped in a subway under Chambers Street on the No. 3 train while the Twin Towers collapsed on top of us. My experience as a survivor and a longtime citizen of Ground Zero, before trauma forced my family to move to Princeton, and even after, as compounded traumas took away my first marriage (which I desperately desired to save), has taught me what metanoia means in my bones. In the daily ritual back then of going every day from my loft three blocks from where the Twin Towers stood to my studio, ten blocks north, I had to come home to Ground Zero. That was my daily "re-pentence," a true journey of metanoia to return home. To do that, I had to face Ground Zero realities in front of me and choose to return to that devastation. Our journey into the light is often through the Ground Zero of our lives.

Art ultimately is an act of intuitive peacemaking, or at least a peace-nest created by grace, a fragile tabernacle of hope in a nomadic desert of despair, a feast in a scarcity-filled world.[13] A scarcity mindset refuses to acknowledge the possibility of beauty in every instance, especially breathing in wasteland toxicity. Culture war originates through that limited view, through a fear-dominated lens. An abundant mindset, one filled with culture care generativity, will see a fragment of hope in Ground Zero, sparkles of fragments embedded within ashes.

I became an artist to focus on those fragments of hope toward the light of abundance. Many told me that this path was impossible. And the art world, especially in the most influential cities of the world, turned out to have values quite the opposite of seeking that light or the movement of *charis*. The art world and technology create a frenzy of hyped interest in transactional market schemes. Artists are often the pawns of such a system, forced to eke out a living from a scarcity model, a world of ego-filled survivor games, or worse yet, part of money-laundering or human-trafficking schemes. As an artist, I then journeyed into my world of faith, into the church, to find a refuge from such zero-sum games, but the result was to find in the churches smoldering reminders of a cruel mechanism of oppression, and, often, the suppression of abuses.

In churches, we learn of the Prince of Peace, Jesus, speaking out of God's abundance, calling all of us to "consider the lilies" (Matt 6:28) instead of being mired in anxiety and fear. Instead, what I found even in the best churches was still a scarcity mindset operating especially among leaders: a message of zero-sum power games lurking beneath the message of hope.[14] In recent times, the church has imitated culture rather than influencing culture. Churches became worlds of power spectacles, creating secret power chambers to hide moral failures and protect abusers in leadership. As I continue to meander to find the Spirit of God, to find elusive beauty lurking outside of the two power systems that I am supposed to belong to, Jesus has guided me in an exilic journey, leading me to experience God's sacred Presence in the studio. What I find strange, and my journey is always evidenced with grace, is that I am a border-stalker who is called to speak back into both worlds of significant tribal realities, the church and the art world, tribal "homes" from which I feel exiled.

Art making can create a space and time for seeking deeper realms of meaning in our complex journey of life and can invite the Prince of Peace to join in the liturgy of making. Such a presence can give agency to peace seekers—those who dare to seek out my paintings as viewers. Peace, to me, defined by the Hebrew word *shalom*, means so much more than lack of violence. Peacemaking is also different from peacekeeping[15]—an understanding that did not come easily to me, just as neither peace nor art comes easily. Shalom signifies the fullness of generative abundance flowing into our scarcity-ridden lives. To create true, lasting shalom, we must train our imaginations to trust our intuition toward integration, toward searching for, and creating, beauty. And, ultimately, this integration is the work of a community that creates peace, justice, and beauty.

I reflect on this fragile beauty, in conflicted and increasingly violent times, as I step inside my studio. In the summer, carpenter bees follow me, their menacing buzz indicating not harm, as they do not sting, but only their territorial insistence. As I shut the glass door, a hush descends, and my studio becomes a sacred place. The converted horse barn has a poured concrete floor, a floor now full of colors from exuberant drips and spilled flows of paint over the years. The original beams are intact, protruding ribs from the drywall ceiling. Sound resonates within, almost womblike, with muted echoes of the pulsating aluminum doors shuddering behind me like heartbeats.

I immediately ponder my next stroke. But I know that the first task is to take a deep breath and slow myself down. The first act of a ritual I go through to prepare to paint is to create a fresh batch of hide glue, in a stick form melted in well water in a double boiler in the back of the studio. Every material points the way to a generative path.

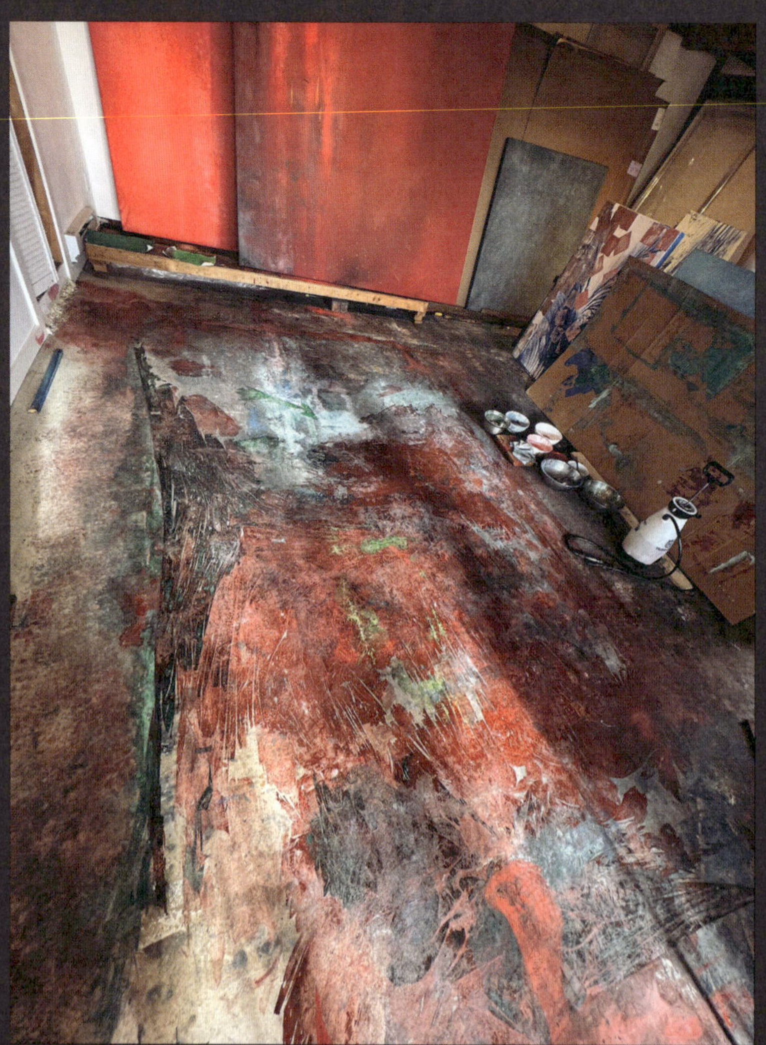

Fuji Farm studio floor after painting.
Copyright © 2023 Makoto Fujimura.

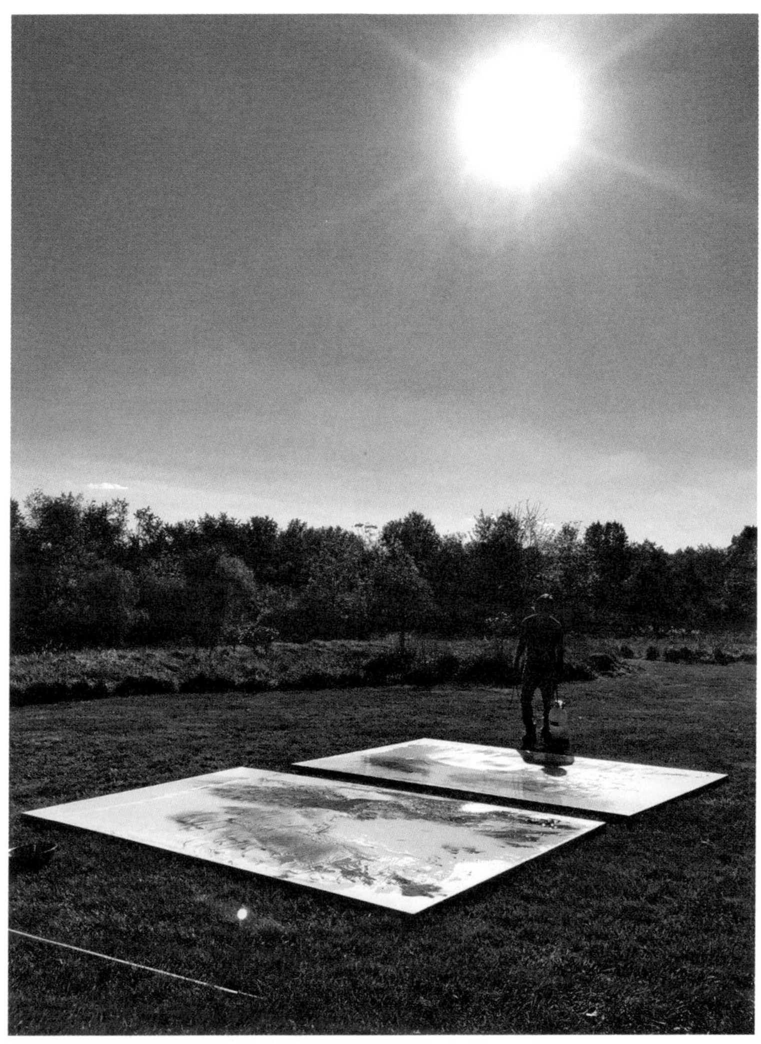

Makoto Fujimura painting *Walking on Water* series, 2021.
Photo by Haejin Shim Fujimura.

The Medium of Making

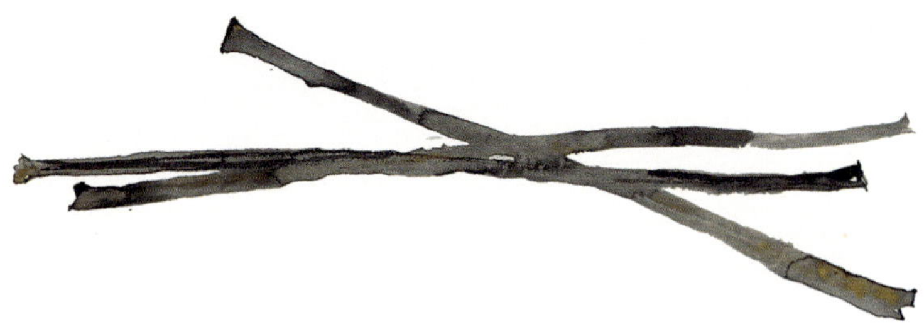

"Sanzenbon" illustration, sumi ink on paper.
Copyright © 2024 Makoto Fujimura.

Japanese *Nikawa*, a traditional glue for use in Nihonga and many other Japanese arts and crafts, is made from cow bones and hides; it is used for layering finely pulverized minerals on paper.[16] Hide glue, perhaps, is the one medium that is used in all cultures as a natural binder, and it comes from hundreds of different sources (including kosher glue made from fish bones) from different cultures. One binder that was commonly used in Japan is *sanzenbon Nikawa*, literally "three thousand sticks of glue." Sanzenbon stopped being manufactured several years ago, before a group of Nihonga masters researched, and advocated for, a new form of the traditional glue sticks by collaborating with chemists to resurrect it from oblivion.

Traditionally, hide and bones were boiled in a vat, then cooled to be solidified and extracted and cut into three thousand sticks.

I take the new sticks of sanzenbon Nikawa into my hands from the shelf and consider their history. When I was a graduate student three decades ago, my mentor told me that the quality of the glue was declining. Sanzenbon Nikawa's resurrection was one rare sign of cultural rejuvenation, an effort to keep this thousand-year-old tradition alive, and I gratefully hold these sticks in my hand every morning; they represent a collaborative merging of art and science.

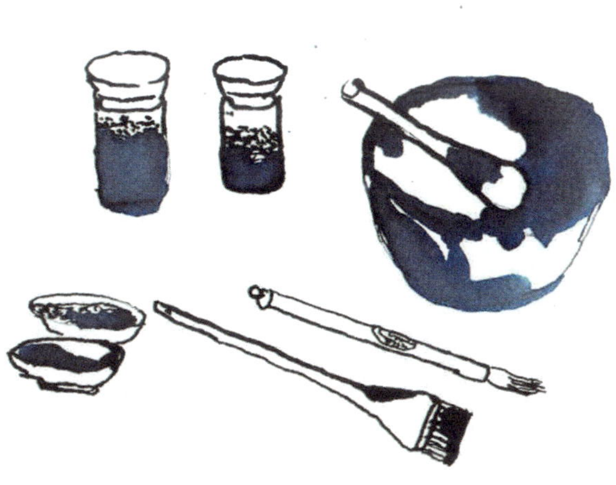

"Nihonga Materials" illustration, from Makoto Fujimura's "Re-Sonance" exhibit booklet, December 2021. Copyright © 2021 Makoto Fujimura.

Nikawa is prepared by first breaking the sticks in a towel before melting them in warm water inside a double boiler. A thick towel is needed to protect your hands from the sharp edges of broken shards. In my morning ritual of breaking the glue sticks, I hear the sanzen-bon sticks cracking, and I know how moist the air is. I then adjust the amount of water, depending on the sound and on the layering I desire to do that day. As my hands feel the breaking of the sticks through a towel, they already know the weather and the temperature, and perhaps even the shifting front of a weather pattern. Just like the thick, moist air of June tells diving tree swallows that rain is coming, my materials bring news of nature's bidding.

Nikawa lasts only several days before spoiling. I've found, though, that the spoiled Nikawa is perfect for some plants as a fertilizer, so my window plants, as well as vegetables outside the studio, benefit from Nikawa. Nothing is thrown away. My art and my tomatoes are fed by ancient Japanese hide glue. Ultimately, my wife and I are also fed by the resilient culture of Japan.

BUDDHIST PRACTICES AND ETHOS forbid the eating and killing of animals. In a Japanese history dominated by Buddhist heritage, one might not be surprised to learn that making this glue from animal hides is a violation of Buddhist ethics. So how did Nikawa become such a central part of art and craft making in Japan?

"The medium is the message," said the media ecologist Marshall McLuhan, and the history and story of Nikawa tell the complex history of Japan, its aesthetics and race struggles. Art has its internal logic and flow, and that logic and flow are literally determined by the medium we use. The medium dictates and defines the boundaries of expression, and its possibilities. The medium, in this case Nikawa, carries the confluence of hidden realities of what Japanese culture poses to the world. In that sense, to understand Nikawa, and its history, is to understand Japanese culture.

The need for such basic materials contributed to upholding a caste system in the shadows of Kyoto culture. *Burakumin,* generations of outcast families, were asked to do what others would not want or be allowed to do: touch the remains of dead animals and create everything from drum skins to Nikawa. Many of the Burakumin were either criminals or forced immigrants from China or Korea, or even, I suspect, the indigenous tribe of Ainu, who lived in Japan before the migration ever began along the Silk Road flowing eventually into Japan. I've found that such things in Japan are only whispered in the dark and are never found in books. When I speak of such things as an outsider (I am considered to be not really Japanese, despite my Japanese parents), I get puzzled looks in Japan, or, worse yet, rejection. But art seeks truth, and even the revealed invisible threads of a hidden past can weave into the new light.

Reveal What Is Hidden

Thus, breaking the Nikawa in my hands, I sense the history of the marginalized and oppressed in Japan. I also give thanks to the animals who gave their lives so I can create beauty. Such a breaking

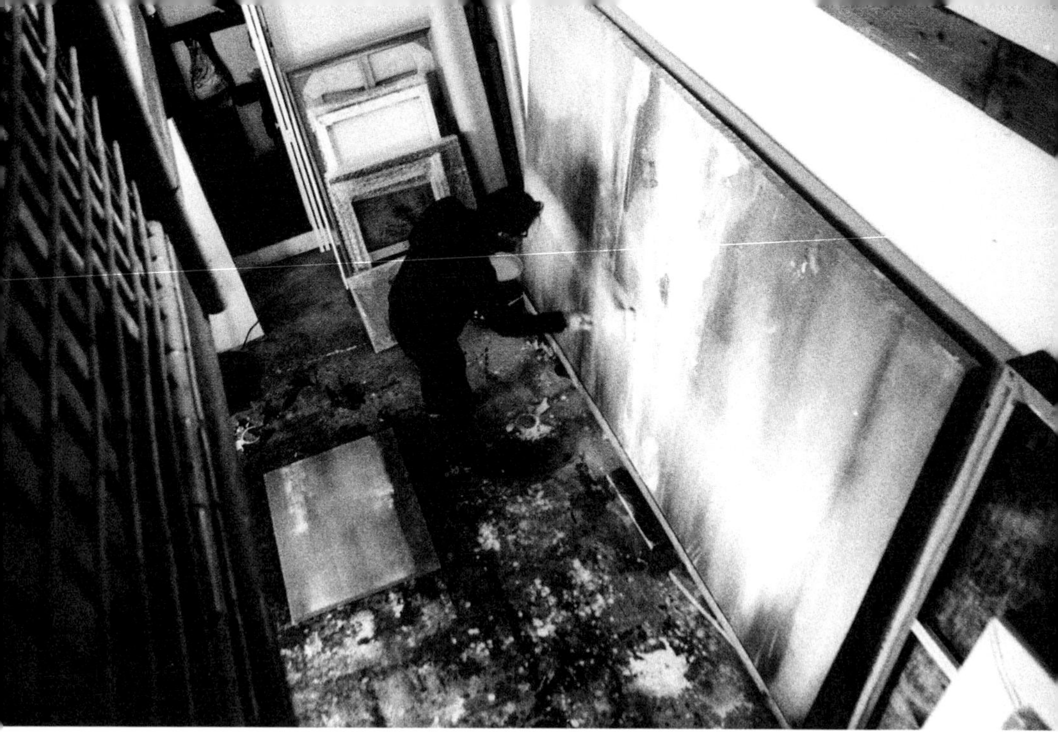

Makoto Fujimura in the studio. Photo credit Alyson LeCroy.

ritual reminds me of how Japanese hidden culture holds (in this case literally, as a glue) the beauty of Japanese art. It is in the fragments that I found the beautiful, and as the shards of sanzenbon Nikawa slowly melt in the double boiler, giving the studio a slightly sweet aroma, I am swimming in the ecosystem of Japanese beauty, both revealed and hidden. My starting point for creating art is the sacrificial gifting and dedication of many generations to make my generative journey possible.

Chapter 2

Listening Room

In our farmhouse, we welcome the visitor to sit down and have a conversation in our Listening Room before or after a brief tour of the studio. Even though it is called a Listening Room, it is focused on visual works rather than music or sound. We have hung one or two paintings in the room, and we serve tea (usually the golden oolong from Taiwan). I speak about the slowness of the process of layering, and even how weather and the moisture level can affect the mixing of paint. It takes about twenty minutes for our eyes and our minds to settle, to be able to "see" a painting.

MY FATHER, Osamu Fujimura, a renowned speech and hearing scientist, told me of the complex connection between information traveling down the optic nerve and auditory nerves. Such journeys between the nerves are meandering and elusive of categories; they have mystified researchers. Our journey into creative spaces, whether in the sciences or the arts, is also meandering and complex. I think of my father every time I sit in the Listening Room.

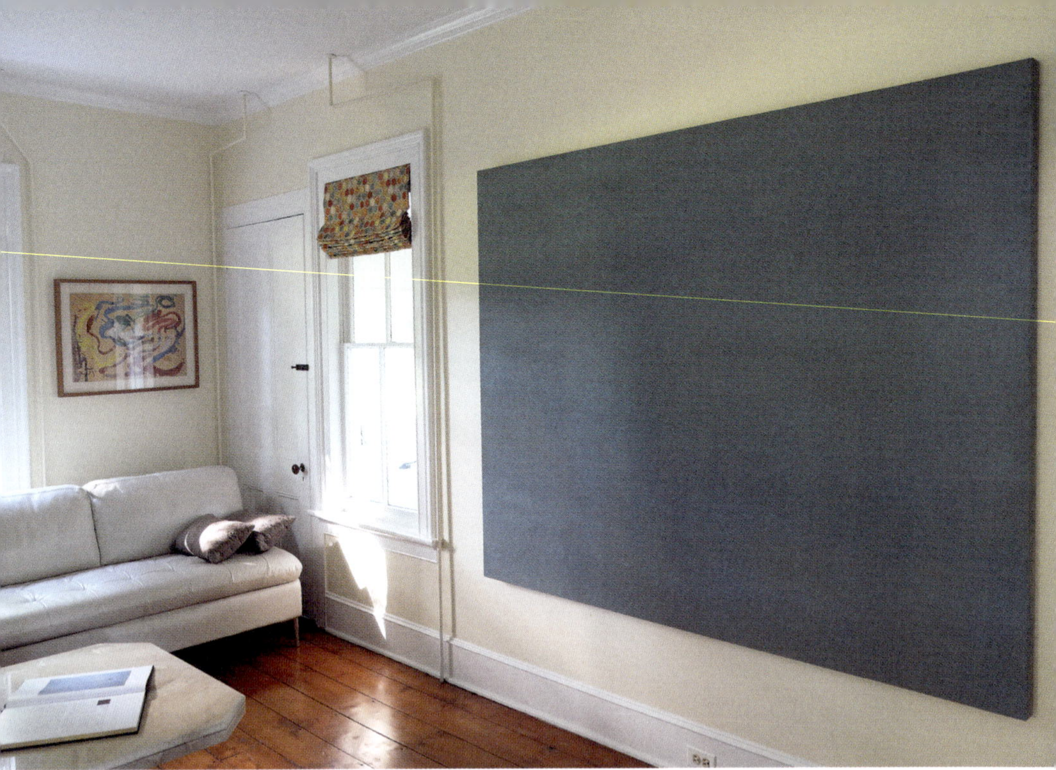

The Listening Room at Fuji Farm. Photo credit Makoto Fujimura.

My father used to sit in front of my paintings for a long time, silent. He and I often spoke of the connection between seeing and listening that comes together in silence. The eye is literally part of the brain, with the optic nerves connected to the deepest parts of the brain, where all senses come together. How the auditory nerves connect cochlear and mid-cortex with the visual stimuli is complex. We still have not gained a full understanding of how these two critical functions of our senses work together. But even in that mystery, my father sat, as a leading acoustics scientist, to try to "hear" my paintings.

Susan R. Barry, an expert in the neuroscience of sight, observes the phenomenon of a blind person being able to see for the first time after an operation:

But where we perceive a three-dimensional landscape full of objects and people, a newly sighted adult sees a hodgepodge of lines and patches of colors appearing on one flat plane. One twenty-five-year-old woman described her first views in this way: "I see an ensemble of light and shadow, lines of different length, round and square things, generally like a mosaic of changeable sensations, that astonish me, and whose meaning I do not understand."[1]

Apparently, similar confusion happens when a deaf person hears for the first time as well. Our senses are not cameras and sound recorders, but processing portals into the myriad of information surrounding us, and our eyes and ears are part of the complex system of neurons and cells that respond collectively to the stimuli around us.

Despite this complexity, in the mysterious deeper realms within the mind, we learn to see. A work of art may be a way to trace how we move from a confusing "ensemble of light and shadow" to a deeper realm of meaning. Art making is a process of mindful self-discovery, as if an artist's "inner eye" can trace the path of sensory input and somatic knowledge. Thus, even if I am painting a landscape, I am paying attention to what the "inner eye" sees. As I try to understand my own process of making, I follow the traces left by somatic making, including my everyday walk into my studio. Thus, even the mundane journey into the studio is intuitively connected with the details of how I give birth to images.

I connect this mystery and complexity to our spirituality. Saint Paul hopes followers of Jesus may experience the eyes of their hearts being enlightened ("I pray that the eyes of your heart may be enlightened in order that you may know the hope to which he has called you, the riches of his glorious inheritance in his holy people" [Eph 1:18 NIV]). Our bodies are connected to our souls. If the brain must learn to interpret complex raw visual stimuli to "see," how much more so the raw spiritual data?[2] Reason and faith have been seen as separate categories and domains, but what if art can bring them together to bear witness to the marvelous intricacies of the deeper knowledge of grace, *charis?* Then, what we call "learning" must include growth as both spiritual and rational beings. Perhaps in educating the whole person, we need to address the totality of our being, including learning to "see with the eyes of our heart." My journey of faith required the deeper connection between poetry, art, and faith.

I have always felt the presence of the divine in the process of making art. My faith is the door of my imagination, as my faith began with "seeing" a poem of William Blake (see "Behind the Veil," Section 1, below). Each of the artists who has influenced me was like a portal into these deeper realities of the integration of rational knowledge and spiritual knowledge.[3]

Seeing Through the Eye

William Blake wrote in the nineteenth century:

> This Life's dim Windows of the Soul
> Distorts the Heavens from Pole to Pole
> And leads you to Believe a Lie
> When you see with, not thro', the Eye[4]

Art is the creation of meaning through our senses. The difference between seeing *with* the eye and seeing *through* the eye is the difference between what machines can detect and what humans can truly "see." It is also the difference between knowledge (*gnosis*) and the deeper knowledge of the soul (*epignosis*). Again, when Saint Paul writes about seeing with the "eyes of your heart enlightened," he is referring to the deepest realm of understanding, and truly seeing *through* the eye. Here at the farm, as the studio of my soul, the senses flow together into a deeper realm of knowing. There is a difference between rote learning and deeper ways of knowing. My art is a portal to help us to connect to this deeper realm of knowledge.[5]

As I navigate the gaps created between the fragments and fissures of culture wars and the art world, I rely on my senses and observe the deeper realm of somatic knowledge that can lead to integration and wholeness. Seeing *with* the eye is to outline, categorize, and even sever information. It is segmented data. My father believed (in the early 1970s) that the segmented data of acoustics research could not

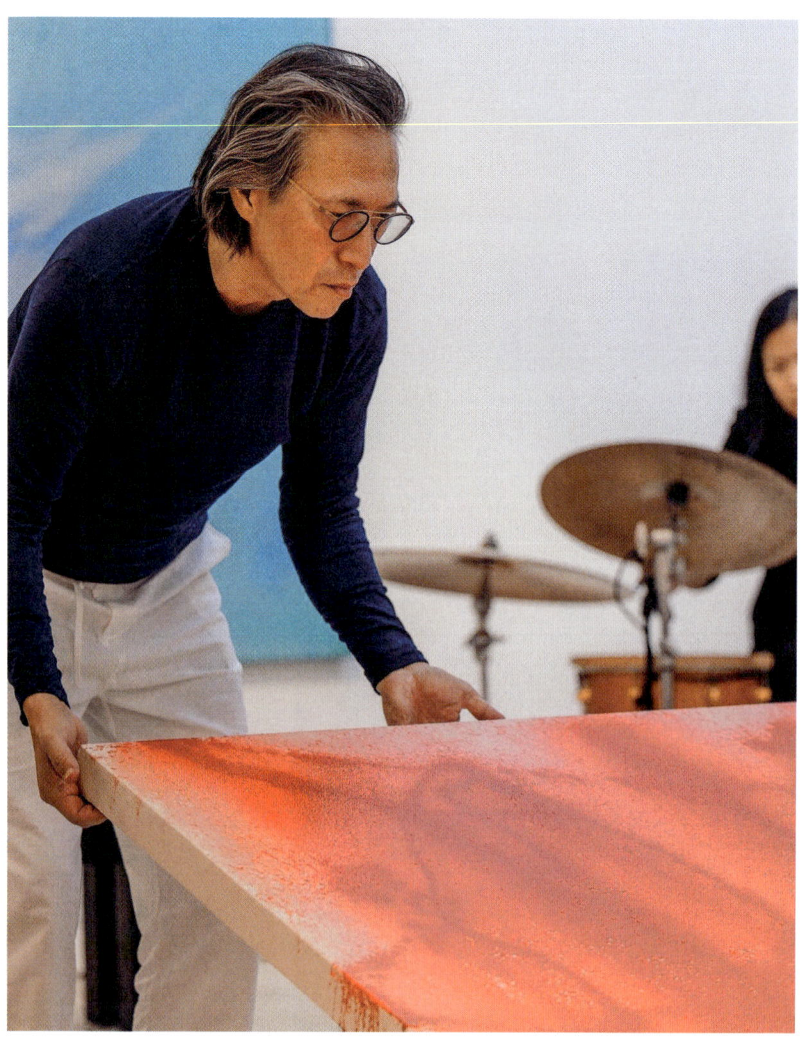

Makoto Fujimura "Live Painting" in collaboration with percussionist
Susie Ibarra, December 2021. Photo credit Windrider Productions.

adequately reproduce human speech. In the same way, how we truly see *through* the eye cannot be done by analysis of segmented visual data (as algorithms of social media platforms do in fragments of bits). Seeing *through* the eye is a holistic, mysterious, deeper realm of processing the nuances of visual reality. To have access to that mystery, we must learn to slow down, to learn to see *through* the eye.

Slow

When a guest sits on the couch in the Listening Room, I explain that it will take at least ten minutes for the overactive brain mechanism to be quiet. First, we are driven to categorize, ignoring overwhelming sensory information flowing in. This is a survival mechanism, filtering to reduce, or even ignore, sensory information so that we can act quickly if need be. Fear and anxiety can further blind us to information coming in. So if, for example, a monochromatic painting such as my *August 30th 19:33,* or a work from my *Blueberry* series is on the Listening Room wall,[6] what we see when we come into the room is only a monochromatic, "abstract" minimalist work with one color on the surface. Sometimes, facing such works, I tell a story, helping the mind to be attuned to reconnect with our senses.

Exile

That day, I was home in my farmhouse, but my heart ached for a true home. For many months, I had been a stranger in my own home, an

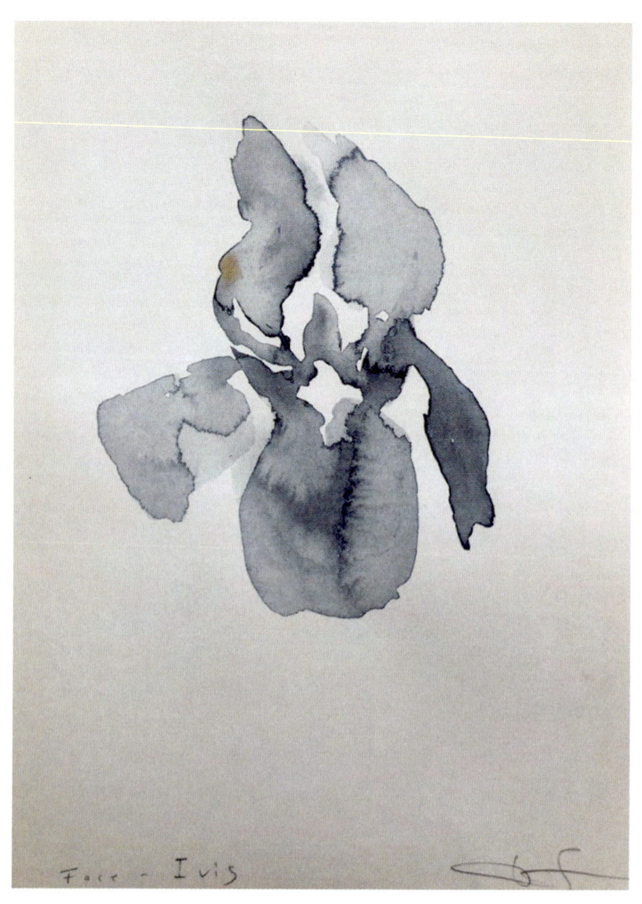

Mercy's Garden Face—Iris, c. 2020, mineral pigments, watercolor, and gold on paper, 12 × 9 in. Copyright © 2020 Makoto Fujimura.

alien in my own body. A series of losses in my life began to erode hope. I was exiled from my own heart's home. My beloved home became a place of exile.

That dark summer, I was working on a "white" painting with no goal in mind; a Sisyphus-like attempt to paint an oyster shell mix on raw Belgium linen. The oyster shell mix goes right through the linen, leaving but a scant ghost of an image behind. The surface does not seem to have much on it after more than 150 layers are applied.

I went into the studio every day to simply have some "meaningless" activity to clear my mind, to pray through my darkness. I was just preparing to settle down for the evening when I felt a sensation overwhelm me, like a thousand feather pillows, soft but prickly, weighing down on top of me. My knees buckled and I was forced to kneel to pray, for how long, I do not know. I know that the sun was setting, and it was completely dark when I opened my eyes.

Not knowing fully what had happened, I staggered to the studio across from my farmhouse. I turned the lights on. There it was, my "white" painting, staring at me, as if it had been waiting for me to arrive. I was startled. Suddenly, its monochromatic white surface—a painting I considered to be not finished—opened the mysteries of what I had just experienced. I had, in some strange sense, painted my "visitation" experience before I had the experience. I felt the prickly sensation again, but this time it was *through* my eyes. My eyes were being opened by the vision and the painting. I could not truly "see" my own painting until the Spirit opened my eyes and my heart, until I fell into the mystery of this deep darkness. It opened the chapel of the mystery and darkness, which signals our true Home.

August 30th 19:33, 2017, oyster shell on Belgium linen, 72 × 116 in.
Copyright © 2017 Makoto Fujimura.

AUGUST 29TH was my father's birthday. He had passed away in the spring of that year—the first year of my life that I could not send a birthday note to him or visit him. My father, the scientist, taught me how to investigate the process of how our hearing works through his acoustics research. In my darkness, I could, finally, "hear" my own paintings. I started to realize, only after his passing, that it was his spirit of authentic inquiry and his refined curiosity that influenced me to do the same, but I applied that in the field of arts and spirituality.

Even though my father was an agnostic, he encouraged me to search for truth and told me that "occidental sciences owe their foundations to Judeo-Christian history." He saw my merging of art and spirituality elevating, as he sat in front to my paintings for literally more than an hour to "hear" the painting. That respect eventually led to my own spiritual inquiry to finding Jesus at the center of my creativity. An agnostic father, therefore, made my Christian faith possible. It was my scientist father who rejoiced that his son wanted to be an artist. My father saw that his artist son would see a world in which gaps of fragmented acoustics data will be filled with gold, and be impervious to the dehumanization of machine language. His pure science led to my art and continues to generatively create into the world.

I told many gallery owners, with whom I worked since then, that no one would understand this painting and we should not exhibit it. No one would stop to see a blank white painting that has no discernible images or even lines. But one keen gallery owner insisted that this painting should be in a museum exhibition. After installing it, I visited the museum without letting people know who I was and stood silently to watch people walk right past this painting, as I had predicted they would. But a few viewers were arrested by it, some teared up before it. I am grateful for these "seers" who took the time to really see my painting.

Defining Your Own Success

Why do I do what I do? Why create beauty? Is it for existential proof of my being? Is it to create a legacy? I ask these questions in the peripheries of my art.[7] I find myself, too, pondering these questions as I work. But ultimately, I am simply painting, like I did as a child, responding and reaching up to communicate the simple joy of how the paint moves on the surface, how I feel like I am "walking on water" when I paint.[8]

These days, slowing down is nearly impossible, with our drive to compete and find "success." We need to take (literally) deep breaths and open our senses. When we recalibrate, we often realize we live without thinking through our motivations. What is success? Not the type of "résumé success" we assume to be the purpose of life. I advise young people to redefine success—"success is when you are able to define your own success." If we are "competing with the Joneses," then such redefinition will not be possible. Art creates a pause to rethink, helping us to slow down, reflect on what we see and hear. Art creates memories that even the ebbing of our physical strength as we age cannot steal away from us. Art can create a different sense of time, moving away from the linear, constant march of *chronos* time,

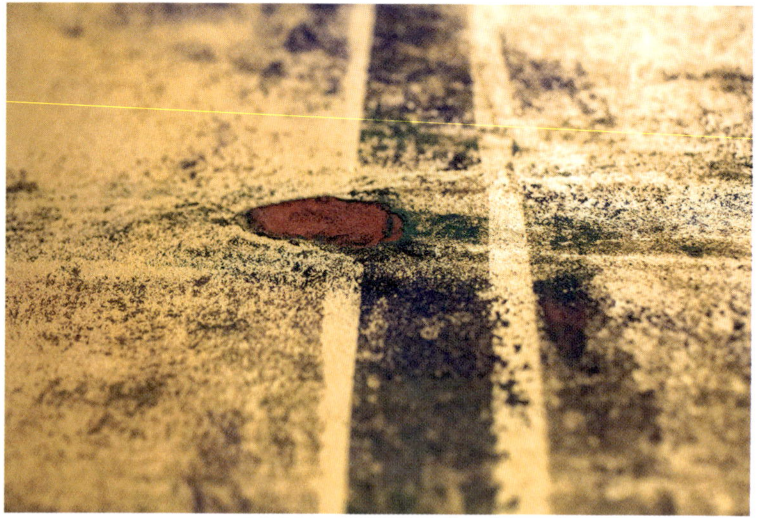

"Wound" detail from *Charis*, 2008, mineral pigments and gold
on Kumohada paper, 89 × 132 in. Copyright © 2008 Makoto Fujimura.
Photo credit Hazel Thompson, 2024.

into being fully Present, into the Time-fulness of every moment, or
kairos time.

When we seek the light, too, there are quicker, seemingly easier
paths. We may gravitate toward neon light like moths, be attracted
to temporary flashes of colors and flames of light that remain for
only a moment. Social media relies on these types of novel flashes
to gain our attention and narrow our focus, reducing our sensory
experiences to bits.

There is an eternal light that reveals and opens the "inner eye."

Traditional liturgies use "perpetual light" (or *lux aeterna*) to consider the journey of those who have passed. Such a notion can be carried into our present lives. Our inner eye may be always aware of such perpetual light, but we are educating ourselves (and being trained through social media algorithms) to not see them, chasing after neon lights.[9] Any great, enduring work of art will transcend the very category in which it was created, to move away from *chronos* to *kairos*. From Greek sculptures to paintings by Agnes Martin or Mark Rothko, when we stand in front of a great artwork, we lose track of time. To accomplish that impossible feat of transcending our momentary survivor mode, great art has always crossed boundaries and defied the neat categorizations that the market demands. The market is a survivor's game; great art endures.

Soon after 9/11, in my Ground Zero studio trying to process the trauma, I listened over and over to a recording that a curator friend sent me of Morten Lauridsen's *Lux Aeterna*.[10] As I have noted in some of my writings about this piece, in such tragic times of incomprehensible loss, only a certain composition can hold the weight of our despair and longing. Enduring art remains because the maker transcends the categories of the marketplace, moving into the vulnerable and sacred realities of our shattered hearts.

My art is therefore made with pulverized remains (literally from prismatic shards of minerals) and painted with tears and ashes (literally with *sumi* calligraphy ink sticks). Many see my art as "abstract," or to be within the category of Nihonga, or simply Japanese painting. I do not think my work fits well in these categories. I am trying to

Lux Aeterna—Hope, 2021, mineral pigments, gold, and gesso on canvas.
Copyright © 2021 Makoto Fujimura.

"essentiate" Reality by focusing on the "Minute Particulars" of pigments to express a greater Reality and by avoiding a reductionist path that defines many conceptual minimalists. So, I am not really an abstractionist or a minimalist.

My work represents a granular attentiveness to a greater Reality, re-presenting that cosmic majesty into the pulverized fragments of the earth. These works are not designed for the established salons of Nihonga, art fairs, or art competitions. They will not be relevant to those who are trying to carve out nationalistic or imperialist propaganda, or to preserve the past in response to the modern, or even to create the new in opposition to the ancient.

My art is an elegiac response to the experience of pulverization, the traumas of our times. Morten Lauridsen wrote *Lux Aeterna* in his experience of grief and loss as well, writing: "I composed *Lux Aeterna* in response to my mother's final illness and found great personal comfort and solace in setting to music these timeless and wondrous words about Light, a universal symbol of illumination at all levels—spiritual, artistic, and intellectual."[11] As an elegiac response, my art is closer to the sixteenth-century Japanese tea master Sen no Rikyū's aesthetic, an aesthetic of lament and repose created during times of feudal war, closer than so much of the art celebrated in the contemporary art scene, or the Nihonga salon scene in Tokyo or Kyoto today. My art is an invitation, a drawn pilgrimage toward a portal into the perpetual light or *lux aeterna*.

Kainos art, what I describe as "New Newness" works from my previous book, will seem transgressive compared with the normative categories of the day and will often create its own category simply because the art will not fit the marketable realm of what is already established. Any "new" art that excites the market tends to be only a temporary flash of transgression, a game to create ridicule in our "attention economy." The more ridicule the "art" brings, such as a banana taped on a wall (which is not about the banana or the tape—art is what art is not), the more the art world places capital ($6.2 million) upon it. *Kainos* art moves beyond the temporary buzz of the contemporary art world into enduring and generative conversation. This is why I look to Rikyū's sixteenth-century tea ceremony, or sado practice, which resonates with the passage from Blake that begins this book: "To see a World in a Grain of Sand / And a Heaven in a Wild Flower." Making *kainos* art is to see beyond the hustle and bustle of our daily lives and to slow down enough to see the infinite in the grain of sand or a heaven in bee balms. To experience the New Creation promised in the Bible, we need a regular liturgy to slow down, to let our senses come alive. We need to meander a bit on the flat stone steps of life, ponder the world around us through the hidden "Minute Particulars," and then enter the studio of our own making.

AFTER SITTING IN A RELAXED SETTING in our Listening Room, our sensory perception begins to open. In a sado session, the tea master is very aware of this. As a participant, one may not immediately notice what type of flower is arranged in the *tokonoma* area of the teahouse, a built-in aesthetic alcove that is designed for flower arrangement and scroll painting or calligraphy. But as the tea master goes through the long "liturgical" process of serving tea,[12] one becomes more awakened to sound and aroma. Then, the taste of a *wagashi* (sweet morsel) given before the tea further awakens our senses, and more importantly, our hearts begin to open.

Sado is slow art. What began as part of a banquet flowing into Japan from the Silk Road became, especially under Rikyū's radical reformation of the tea ceremony tradition, a path of peace in a war-torn nation.[13] Rikyū took the tea ceremony, typically used as part of a banquet of many being served at once, and transformed it into a solitary journey of a guest and a tea master. This, in essence, is what I am trying to create in my art as I journey into my art barn.

Chapter 3

Sen no Rikyū

Hospitality

Sen no Rikyū's aesthetic redefined the Japanese aesthetic. Rikyū renovated what was passed down from Chinese Zen tradition to use the medicinal green pulverized tea leaves in the sado ceremony he developed.[1] Rikyū's tea ceremony is a disciplined ritual requiring the apprentice to spend more than a decade just to begin to master all the minute movements. A meandering path led into his small teahouses, which became smaller and smaller as Rikyū developed his aesthetics. What was once a banquet room eventually became a tiny room of one-and-a-half tatami mats in size (thirty-six by ninety inches), forcing the guest to sit face-to-face with the tea master. It was also Rikyū's invention to create a *nijiriguchi,* a small, square crawl-in entry to the tearoom, which was inspired by the entry into a small river boat. Carefully choreographed details anticipate each pilgrimage to fulfill the invitation given exclusively by the tea master. A nijiriguchi was designed for the visitor to enter through, but a samurai was forced to bow and humble himself to enter the teahouse and, more importantly, had to remove his sword and leave it beside

49

the rock at the entry. The journey into the teahouse is considered just as important as sitting to have tea. In the same way, the path leading up to my studio prepares my heart for the sacred life of being called to be an artist.

My art and the trajectory of my life owe a great deal to Sen no Rikyū. Although I had not been trained in the art of sado, Rikyū's aesthetic and approach to art as peacemaking deeply affected how I viewed my own art and life. My training in Nihonga was, in essence, an effort to understand the history of Japanese art, and to find my voice in the streams of aesthetics flowing out of Rikyū.

Service

Rikyū established his sado, his innovation of the art of tea, during a period of feudal bloodshed in Japan. He literally invented his form of tea to serve and communicate with warlords. Consider the improbability of this act: almost everything Rikyū did to refine the art of tea was an intentional act of peacemaking in a time of brutal dictatorial reigns filled with violence and death. It would be like setting up a teahouse on the borders of Gaza today, offering a time of repose to both Israeli generals and Hamas leaders. The questions that rise naturally: How did he accomplish this, and how did he get away with it?

Francis Xavier (1506–1552) encountered an island beyond Macau, now known as Japan, that had an unusual level of education and literacy.[2] This high literacy no doubt influenced the culture of elites. Many of the warlords Rikyū hosted and served as an advisor were of

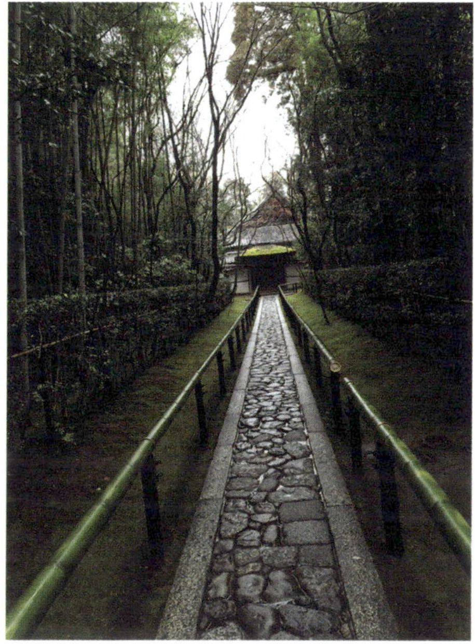

Sen no Rikyū teahouse.
Photo credit Makoto Fujimura.

the educated elite. One most powerful warlord, Hideyoshi, was not educated thus, growing up in a peasant home, perhaps a significant historical note in Rikyū's ultimate demise.

Rikyū's liturgy of tea highlighted the importance of restraint and silence. He mastered the art of *beholding* as a path to communicating peace. Rikyū also intentionally used Korean vessels to serve tea to shoguns and warlords about to invade Korea. This was an act of pressing back against the dictatorial forces that sought to advance

"Tea bowl" illustration, from Makoto Fujimura's "Re-Sonance" exhibit booklet, December 2021. Copyright © 2021 Makoto Fujimura.

their territorial battles into foreign lands. Rikyū so effectively communicated and advocated for peace that he created a liturgy that outlasted the dictatorial Tokugawa shogunate (1603–1868) to today. He also created, perhaps quite intentionally, an underground economy valuing simple elegance and an aesthetic that merged the modest beauty of Korean aesthetics with Japanese refinement.[3] He elevated the craft of his main ceramicist, Chojiro—who was working as an exiled craftsman from China (or Korea) making roof tiles—so much so that Chojiro's tea ware is the most coveted tea ware in Japan today. Of course, such a revered figure would not be allowed to exist in a bloodthirsty land full of aggression.

It is no overstatement to say that Sen no Rikyū is the most venerated figure in Japanese aesthetic history. Almost everything we know and appreciate about Japanese aesthetics flows out of his innovation of refining the Zen legacy and paving a new path for the art of tea. Instead of the perfection of Chinese porcelain, we seek beauty in the broken and worn form of *wabi-sabi* art.[4] *Wabi* means "poverty," and *sabi* means "rust." This humble aesthetic is to be contrasted with the high elegance of the Chinese aesthetic and creates a path for Japanese culture to be akin to Korean culture. Although this idea existed before Rikyū, it was Rikyū's life and death that became the most important symbol of peacemaking in war-torn times.[5] Rikyū, therefore, elevated the wabi-sabi concept into what we know today to be the Japanese aesthetic. His renown became so widespread in the elite society of Japan that his influence became too dangerous for Toyotomi Hideyoshi, and Rikyū was ordered to commit hara-kiri, or seppuku (Japanese ritualistic suicide), with his blood staining the tatami mats of the very teahouse in Kyoto he had designed for peace.[6]

Sacrifice

Through the art of tea Rikyū created a portal into the new realities of Japanese culture, integrating the aesthetics of the East flowing into Japan along the Silk Road. Rikyū's demise (and his many disciples were also persecuted for their faith in Christ) has left an indelible mark, leaving behind an enduring culture of peace. It is curious that it was during Rikyū's era that the severe persecution of Christians began in Japan. As a historical and aesthetic overlap of Japanese wabi-sabi aesthetic with Christian persecution, an object of curse for Christians exists in Japan that has become an emblem of persecution—*fumi-e*.[7]

Fumi-e are "stepping blocks" created during the Tokugawa era to identify hidden Christians living in villages, leading to their arrest and most of the time leading to their deaths. The authorities cast a bronze image of Christ and/or the Virgin Mary onto a block and forced villagers to tread on it to see what their reaction would be. This insidious persecution of Christians lasted more than 250 years, and it left a severe imprint on the culture of Japan. Fumi-e is literally a negative imprint on the psyche of Japanese society, cast improbably with the image of Christ and still today deeply imbedded in the Japanese psyche.

I believe now that Rikyū himself, whose second wife Oriki was one of the converts to Christianity in Kyoto, was a hidden believer. Furthermore, Rikyū created the liturgy of tea (a liturgy not unlike communion in a Catholic Mass) to preserve the sacred act of Christian worship via hidden means. The warlord Hideyoshi recognized this connection. After Rikyū's demise, Hideyoshi ordered that the statue of Rikyū at Daitokuji temple be taken down and "crucified," as Jesus was. In Hideyoshi's mind, Rikyū's art of tea, his influence, and the "dangers" of egalitarian Christian teaching honoring every human being were deeply connected. In 1587 Hideyoshi also ordered the banning of Christianity in Japan, an edict that lasted for more than 250 years.[8]

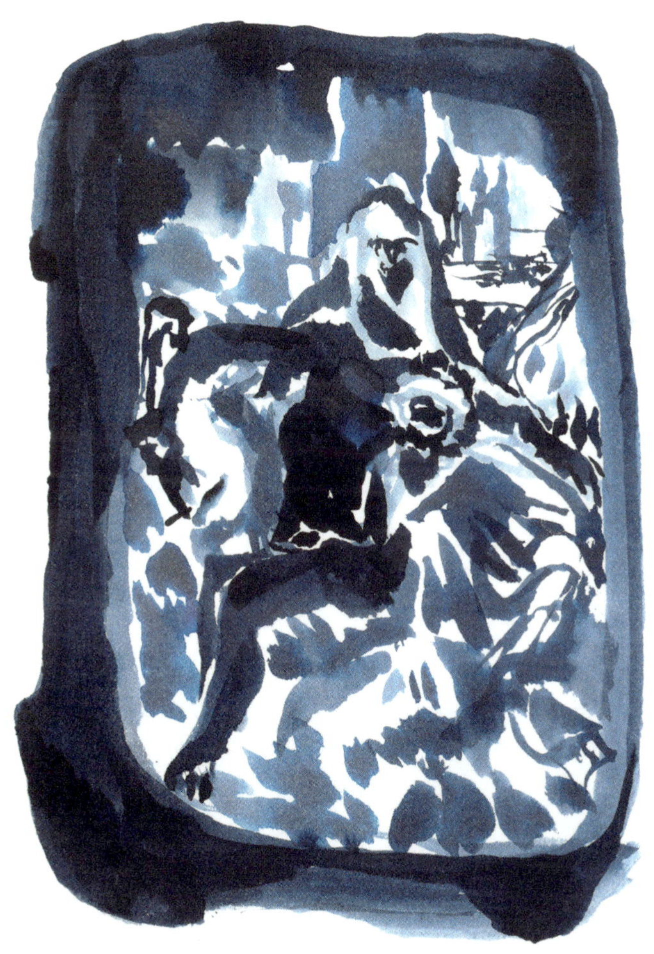

"Fumi-e" illustration, from Makoto Fujimura's
"Re-Sonance" exhibit booklet, December 2021.
Copyright © 2021 Makoto Fujimura.

For centuries after Rikyū's death and throughout the years of Christian persecution in Japan, hidden Christians celebrated communion through Rikyū's style of serving tea. In the famed Buddhist Daitokuji temple in Kyoto where Rikyū is venerated, a hidden teahouse exists that only Buddhist priests knew about. It was marked by Oribe, one of Rikyū's key disciples, with stone lanterns and hidden sculpted images of Mary and the Child underneath the ground. These stone lanterns are now famously called *Oribe toro*, and pieces of Oribe earthenware are full of crosses, both visible and invisible. The hidden Christians followed the lit Oribe lanterns until they joined the private tea ceremony, where they silently observed worship, experiencing a hidden communion.

Fracture

As I meander the stone paths to get to my studio, I am always mindful of Rikyū, with his genius language of peacemaking birthed out of feudal bloodshed. Art follows the meandering, sometimes hidden, path of peace. Peace begins by beholding the fragments of what is broken. As I behold the fragments of the trauma in our days, I also recognize that our path to create beauty today will require particular sacrifice and wisdom. Out of these moments in history flows a language of peace and care that we might learn from today, when brutal dictatorial forces and powerful algorithms may not allow us to speak of these ideals in a straightforward fashion.

Out of this influence of Rikyū, the ancient practice of Kintsugi

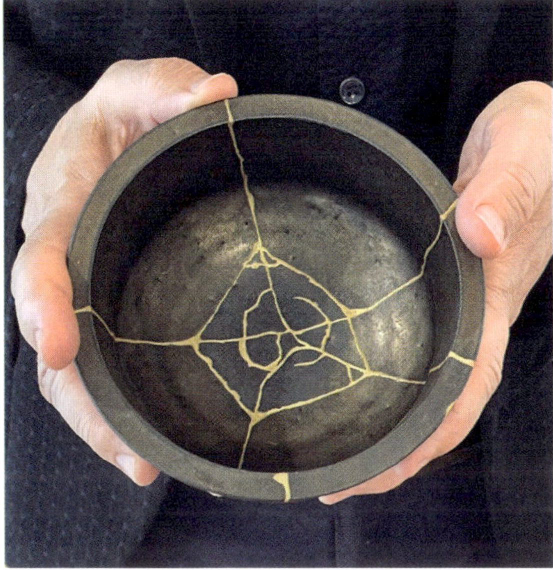

Makoto Fujimura holding an ancient Japanese ceramic vessel mended with Kintsugi. Photo credit Windrider Productions.

flowed. Kintsugi is a venerable tradition from Korea and Japan of mending broken ceramics with lacquer and gold. The Kintsugi tradition is related to the tea ceremony as the *urushi* (a traditional Japanese lacquer made from poison sumac trees) creates a bond of the mended parts to be even stronger than the original material. *Kin* means "gold" in Japanese, and *tsugi* means "to mend"; *tsugi* also means to connect generations. The resulting mended Kintsugi bowl is more valuable than the original because it has been through two master's hands—one who made the ceramic and one who mended it.

Can we enter the sacred through the imperfect and broken, rather than pretending to be perfect and unbroken and seeking to "win" at all costs? What if art is a path that honors brokenness and allows the light to shine through the cracks? What if art is where the divine Presence is expressed through weakness and vulnerability, rather than through power and invulnerability? Such is the path of Rikyū, transposed in the art of Kintsugi and, by extension, in my own works. On such a humble path, we are not exulting the painful journey of becoming broken. We do not celebrate being shattered or dis-abled. We are not surrendering rights to defend our territories to be abso-lute pacifists. As a result of having culture wars out of our scarcity mindset, as well as lacking the stewardship of imagination toward beauty, we cannot celebrate our longings today. But even if we can-not celebrate, we can yet behold. The family of a Kintsugi master or tea master will behold the broken fragments for several generations as stories are passed down of a broken vessel used in an important tea ceremony.

Art can also be a place where everyone's broken journey is hon-ored and beheld until each of the broken pieces can be beautiful unto themselves. In Kintsugi, beauty and justice can coexist, as the master restores the broken and yet beautifully creates the new as an emblem of all our journeys forward. Our journey into the light is through such brokenness and cracks. Traumas can give birth to art.[9]

For the twentieth commemoration of the 1999 massacre at Col-umbine High School, I gifted the school a Kintsugi vessel (a seven-teenth-century Korean tea bowl mended in Japan in the nineteenth

Columbines—Hope (detail), 2021, mineral pigments, silver,
and oyster shell on Kumohada paper, 48 × 72 in.
Copyright © 2021 Makoto Fujimura.

century) and a small silver Columbine painting. The painting was a work I began in lament over the mass shooting, the first of many to come. I had done a series of Columbine paintings in 1999 with oyster shell *gofun* on silver, and I rediscovered a few panels that I had started then but not finished.

The work I gave to Columbine High School is of delicate columbine flowers sitting in the shade of pine trees in Colorado mountains in the summer, almost transparently white, rather than the bright purple petals they become in the sun. Translucent petals were a perfect symbol of vulnerable young souls wafting in the shadows of the sun. Gofun is a material that perfectly captures the translucent and yet luminous white.

When my gallery asked what dates should be used to archive the painting, I answered "1999–2019." The work I had started and put away, I was able to complete for the twentieth-anniversary gift. It took twenty years to finish that one painting. But perhaps I should have noted the painting dates as "1999–?," as the silver will continue to tarnish, and as the paintings darken the white translucent petals, by contrast, will become brighter and brighter.

My art uses pulverized minerals to create a somatic visual portal. Through the brokenness of mineral shards, we dive into the refractive light. To behold refractive light is to see that broken fragments can lead to abundance and draw us out toward the eternal light.

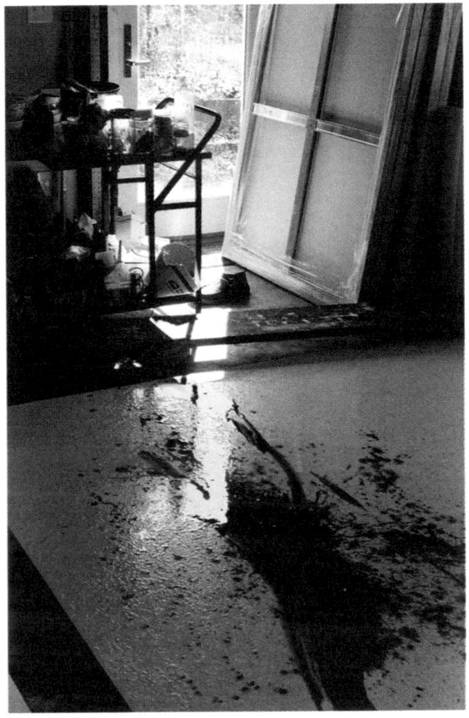

A painting drying in the studio.
Photo credit Alyson LeCroy

Beholding

Jesus, an itinerant rabbi in first-century Palestine, insisted, "Love your enemies and pray for those who persecute you" (Matt 5:44). He taught this in the most insecure, violent lands, with many factions fighting over them. This "impossible command" to "love your enemies" in such a place challenges us. Jesus is reframing our cate-gories—to live with radical generosity and think in an "upside down," counterintuitive, and even paradoxical fashion. He is asking us to be artists. It takes imagination to love.

For those listening to Jesus in the Galilee hills, there was no guar-antee for the future, no health insurance to cover illnesses. There was no Israeli government or US missiles to protect the Jews, and the threat against any minority group was imminent. So why would this voice call out to say, "Blessed are the poor in spirit"? This determined path toward this "impossible peace" is our journey into the light, a path this book is dedicated to. How do you begin to cherish those who have hurt you, traumatized you, and even destroyed your life? Did Jesus mean a blanket forgiveness that allows evil to take over, and did he mean that we should do nothing to prevent evil? Did he mean to passively watch evil take over?

Jesus also gave his life "as a ransom for many" (Mark 10:45), as he warned his disciples. I walked about the path surrounding the Sea of Galilee pondering how Jesus saw the hills overlooking the water. Today, smoke from bombing on the Syrian hills can be seen from there, with constant threats from Hezbollah missiles.

On the same hillsides where Jesus taught this impossible com-mand to "love your enemies," he also gently commanded his follow-ers to "consider the lilies" and "look at the birds of the air." If we want to consider and look, we may want to draw them. We may appropri-ately wonder, What does being attentive to fragile beauty around us have to do with loving our enemies? Jesus is commanding us to do so.

RIKYŪ CONSIDERED the lilies. Rikyū, in his own way, began to develop a liturgy for such "impossible peace" during a time of feudal warfare in Japan. Wabi-sabi aesthetics literally defined "the poor in spirit," represented in tea ware. Cherry blossoms are most beautiful when they are falling; maple leaves are at their brightest when they are dying. Art rises above the time and place it's made, becoming a portal for us to ponder how impossible dreams might become actualized. What Jesus brought about in his "upside-down Kingdom" was a harbinger of how so many human beings have attempted the impossible, even though all of them suffered as mortals.

Such sufferings require a different mode of observation to arrive at beauty—a time of forbearance; times of great strife and bloodshed require the discipline of beholding.

Stewardship of Nature

Kintsugi depends upon the indispensable medium of urushi, a lacquer made from Japanese sumac. Japanese urushi is notoriously difficult to master, and even before one begins to use it, one must test one's immunity to the poison sumac, as a third of the population is highly allergic to it. Many students in an urushi class will not be able to go beyond the first semester of the lacquer major at Tokyo University of the Arts because of the severe rashes they develop. Pursuit of such elegant beauty accompanies such risks.

Furthermore, the best urushi trees, found in the northern mountains of Japan, are specifically raised by generations of urushi har-

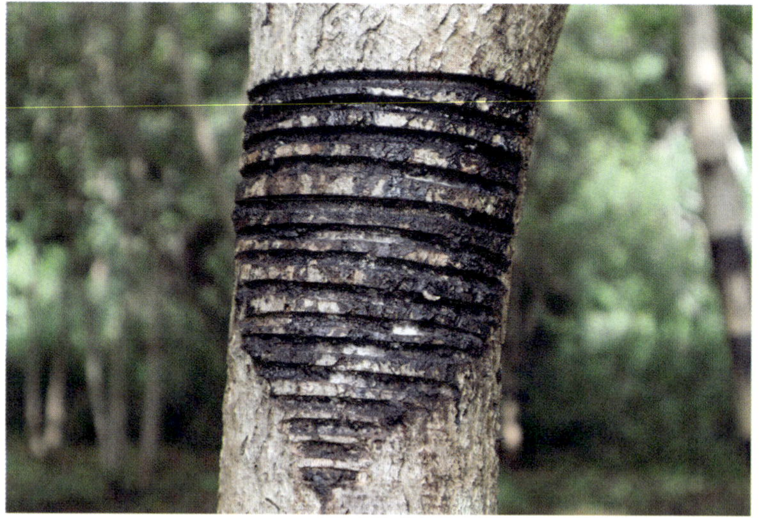

Urushi tree scars. Copyright © 2021 Toru Tsuji, photograph by Kana Goto.
Reprinted by permission of Toru Tsuji. I am grateful to urushi master
Keisuke Sano for these photos and details of urushi harvest.

vesters. The tree in the colder climate of the north does not grow as fast as its southern counterparts in Asia. Because of this slow growth, a tree can give only two hundred grams of urushi, through carefully orchestrated cuts, with only twenty to twenty-five cuts allowed per season. Then they will be cut down, to wait for new growth, which will take ten years before additional cuts can be made. Urushi oozes out slowly from each horizontal cut and oxidizes into reddish sap. Such precious Japanese urushi is therefore more expensive than gold.

"Urushi trees give their life blood so we can create beauty," a young urushi master told us. An audible gasp filled the air as we saw photos of a cut urushi tree. It reminded us of the Bible passage:

> But he was pierced for our transgressions,
>> he was crushed for our iniquities;
> the punishment that brought us peace was on him,
>> and by his wounds we are healed.
> We all, like sheep, have gone astray,
>> each of us has turned to our own way;
> and the LORD has laid on him
>> the iniquity of us all. (Isa 53:5–6 NIV)

The Japanese lacquer technique is one of the most refined crafts to come out of Japan. As one trained in Nihonga, and not in urushi, I can only guess at the level of difficult patience required to master this art form. Urushi is not just used in closing the gaps created in broken vessels, but as a varnish that results in the elegant earth-red to black color that Japanese lacquer is known for. When I watch urushi masters work, I see years of sacrifice behind every gesture, and their humility to serve the "life blood" of urushi trees—a life that comes through delicate layers of a thousand-year tradition. As I watch them, I connect the beauty of their work with the suffering of nature toward the creation of beauty.

Such suffering, in my mind, is cut and drawn into the hands of the one who claimed to be the Creator, Christ's blood flowing into the fabric of Creation.[10] The resurrected Jesus looked like a gardener

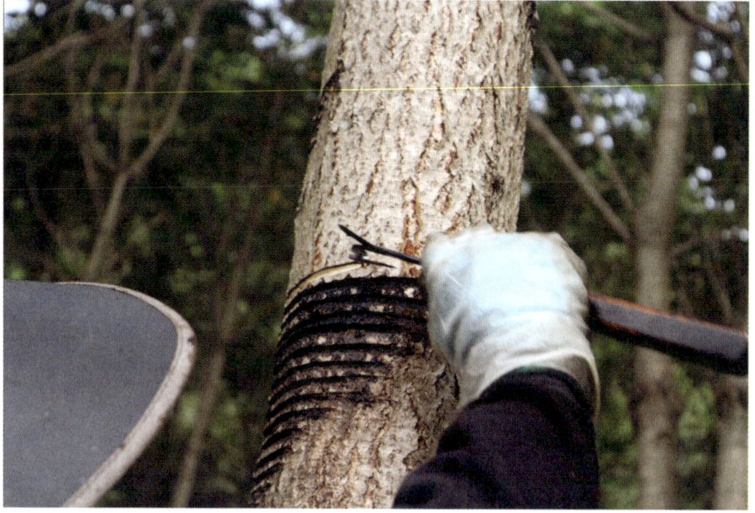

Urushi tree sap being collected. Copyright © 2021 Toru Tsuji, photograph by Kana Goto. Reprinted by permission. Photo courtesy of Keisuke Sano.

to Mary. Perhaps in a mysterious way, we all know that such divine sacrifice and invitation to the New Garden/City will require a Gardener/Savior. Perhaps we need to learn to cultivate precious trees for several generations to understand what sacrifice is required to create beauty. All creativity, likewise, involves generational giving. Beauty is not birthed overnight and is given as grace through broken, imperfect realities.

Are we, too, a mosaic of broken shards, reconnected and redrawn by the Creator, the ultimate Kintsugi master? Again, I ask—What if our communities are seen as fragments brought together for a peace

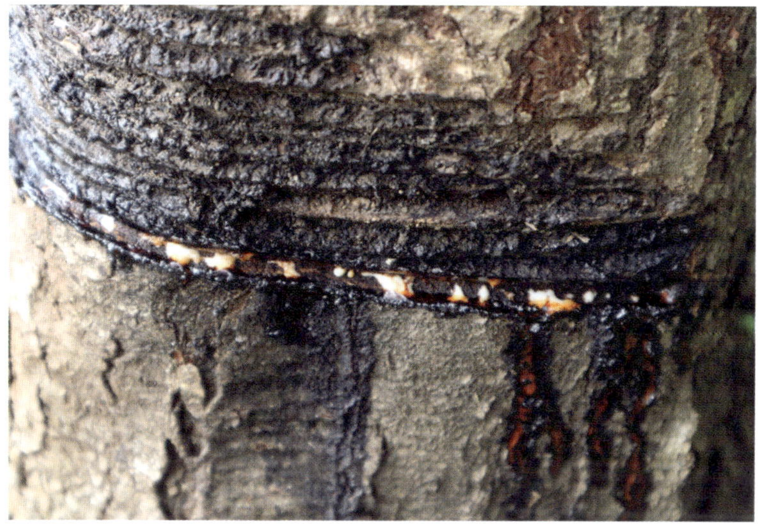

Urushi tree "weeping." Copyright © 2021 Toru Tsuji, photograph by Kana Goto. Reprinted by permission. Photo courtesy of Keisuke Sano.

offering to our violent world?[11] Wounds, whether they be those of an urushi tree or those of Christ, are portals into the miraculous sacrifice that leads to beauty. Proper generational stewardship can turn even poison into beauty.

Yobi-tsugi

Yobi-tsugi further extends the Kintsugi technique of mending into a complex and beautiful mosaic. The yobi-tsugi method intentionally brings together a fragment from a foreign vessel to fill in a missing

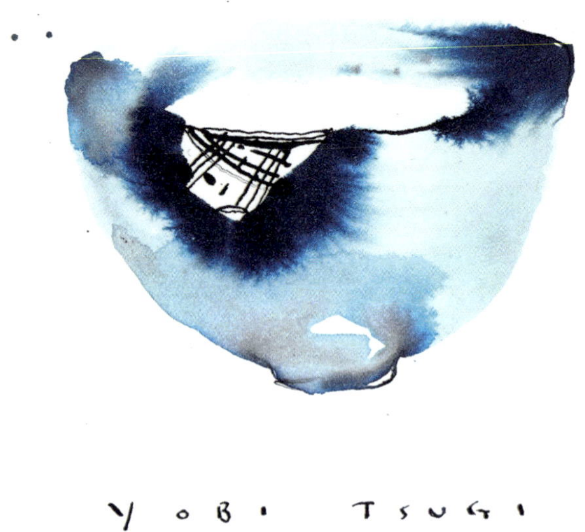

"Yobi-tsugi" illustration, from Makoto Fujimura's "Re-Sonance" exhibit booklet, December 2021. Copyright © 2021 Makoto Fujimura.

piece. *Yobi* means "to call," and this Kintsugi master will bring two cultures together—often warring ones, such as Korea and Japan or Pakistan and India, sometimes with the broken edges mimicking the geographical borders of the two countries in conflict—as a peacemaking journey, to literally envision peace.

Painting with Nihonga minerals here in America reminds me of the yobi-tsugi process, an intentional patchwork of different minerals of varying weights and pulverized patterns of coarseness, in many layers, ultimately finding unexpected resonance. In my case, I mix in space-age materials that accommodate the drier air of Princeton. Here, instead of "filling in" the fragments, by *yobi-komu* they "call in" challenging combinations, sometimes playfully calling in unexpected combinations.

I, too, in my paintings, create intentional tension within the work by pairing materials that often "fight" against each other. Japanese vermillion will tarnish silver leaf underneath. Even in the use of silver, waiting (sometimes for decades) for the surface to settle and tarnish results in works that capture the changing process of time. In using silver, with the intention of seeing the years marked in the tarnishing surface, I am painting time itself by capturing, over many years, the ever-changing patina. A surface can capture the years of subtle shifts, often resulting in calling (*yobi*) in layers of time in a single surface.

Additionally, thematic motifs are also juxtaposed, such as images of flames painted with water (*Water Flames*) or beachlike patterns created by gravity to create solidity, but the patterns look like waves (*Walking on Water*). The dry atmosphere of California, when I had a second studio there, created a pattern of "lifting" of fast-drying layers of heavy minerals under a hot sun, resulting in the dry heat creating a pattern of that lifting. Each art marks location and time. All art can be yobi-tsugi, the "calling" of various materials together, and stewarding that ethos of mosaic, blending to behold together.

Kintsugi and yobi-tsugi are more than the craft and skill of restoring and renewing ceramics; they can also be a lifestyle or cultural language to value. What they teach leads into what I have termed the "generative thinking and living" of culture care.[12] This is a pattern of thinking and making that is born out of resilience, even when one is surrounded by violence and strife. Such a lifestyle offers a path out of a scarcity mindset. Artists can lead in this way of generative life. By making, and by living a "Kintsugi life," artists can lead in "loving our enemies."

"What we behold, we will become," the spoken word artist Joshua Luke Smith eloquently stated.[13] To behold is to love. To love those who persecute us, we must first know them enough to behold them as they are, and to understand what causes such anger to be directed at us or someone else. By beholding, we do not accept current realities; by beholding, we become who we ought to be. Such a patient path requires courage and discipline, being faithful to thinking beyond what is normative and conventional. Whether that "thinking beyond" happens in a jail in Birmingham, Alabama, or on Robben Island, South Africa, or in the sixteenth-century blood-soaked land of Japan, prophetic voices of history teach us by making and writing beyond the walls of intolerance and dictatorial oppression. I consider courageous people such as Dr. Martin Luther King Jr., Nelson Mandela, and Rikyū to be great artists.

The first thing that an artist must do is to define and depict the light coming out of darkness. Darkness is the canvas of life in which light emerges, creating boundaries so we can see. We are born into darkness, and we navigate the complex, if not traumatizing, world of light. Every single person coming out of the womb of a mother experiences the trauma of birth. We come out of darkness into the light.

As I walk the stone path to my studio, even before I lay down a single layer of mineral pigments, my heart longs for prismatic illumination, a gentle stream of light that I already saw in the Milky Way on a crisp autumn night. It took me nearly five years to truly begin to "understand" this place where I live. Now, when I am traveling, I miss the farmland as much as I may miss a friend. These three acres of land have become a portal through which I can see the entire universe. This deep, intimate connection with the land, the care for each detail that resonates even during our travels, is a path laid out in every tea garden in Japan. A garden, even a stone garden, requires constant attention and care.

I am beginning to understand that intimacy of care through watching bluebirds nest or French oregano spread its aromatic tentacles. That intimacy is linked with my own deeper journey through my darkness, and the "flow" of what my art connects me to. There are gaps in between, just like the stone steps, in the gaps of which I have poured sand so that it is a bit easier to weed. But such gaps are also sacred, as in Kintsugi fissures, spaces to behold, and envision a new reality.

I ponder the connections between the disparate elements of what I see here, between the stones and the grassy lands I let grow wild, between the fences and the preserved land beyond, between the farmhouse and the barn, between the stars and the minute grains of pulverized minerals. My art journey tells me that there are distinctive elements, such as the Nihonga materials I use or the different languages I write with, that are separated by gaps, but there are more overlaps than areas of clear separation. Art can playfully explore such unique discoveries in the margins.

Chapter 4

Art as Play

I step on the wet sands of Kamakura beach, waves caressing my feet, the sands shifting underneath. I am being lulled into a greater force— the forces of the undertow, waves perhaps initiated long ago in far- away seas, gravitational forces of the moon drawing up and enticing the surface tensions.

Every summer day in my childhood, my mother walked me up and down the hills of Inamuragasaki in Kamakura, an ancient cap- ital (1185–1333), to swim in a moss-green-water outdoor pool, then to walk along Yuigahama beach. One morning, a fishing boat, with cerulean blue edges, was coming in with nets full of fish and other shiny creatures wiggling and refracting into a rainbow dance. After a tantalizing hour of observing them, I came home and painted them.

I realized only later that my mother had always made a place for me to paint, as if that would be the most natural thing for a child to do. My imagination was full of creatures of the deep, an enchantment caught in the fine hand-woven nets, and I could relive that wonder- ment over and over on watercolor papers. I tried to be faithful to what I saw, fish of various kinds, red snappers, sardines, and anchovies, but also mini octopuses and large starfish and iridescent clam shells mixed in, all glistening in the shifting morning light, and fishermen's wrinkled hands and women with purple *furoshiki* hair-covers bending low to scoop the creatures up with bamboo baskets.[1] All these memories I have tried to capture through painting, even today.

Childhood is the foundation for our art. Memories from our earliest days are the material for our journey into the light.

Memories have eyes that can see beyond the sea. Seeing through the eyes of the heart means cultivating an awareness for the gift of life, past and present. Such a gift, like the gifts of shiny creatures from the sea, can open our hearts toward that joy we once knew, and the sense of play that every moment can bring. Art is a path to receive and cultivate the gift (*charisma*) of life. Art is simply to pay attention to these small miracles, and to create into them with childlike faith.

I recall painting as a child. I remember feeling this energy flow through me. The hair on the back of my neck stood up, and a charge traveled straight into my hands, through the tips of my fingers into my brush. I did not know what to call that experience, which I assumed everyone had.[2]

My mother kept a painting that I did when I was three years old, and it has the same flow, the same sequence of colors and gestures that I use today. It is now in the Listening Room. It was not until I was in my late twenties that I connected that experience of the "flow" with the Word in the Bible. The words of Christ and the Psalms came to me as an eternal song, a resonance I felt beyond my limited existence. These profound connections helped me bridge what seemed

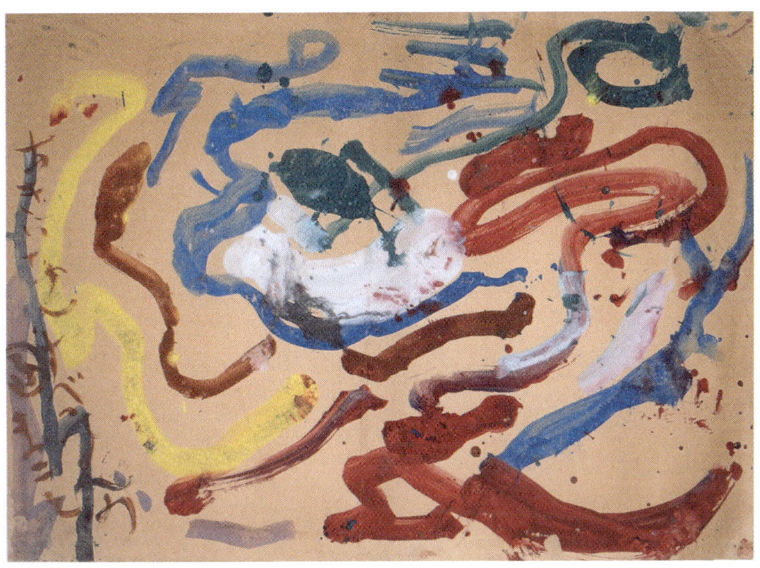

Makoto Fujimura's "three-year-old painting."
Copyright © 1963 Makoto Fujimura.

like unbridgeable gaps between faith and creativity, East and West, painting and writing, and they launched me on a new journey (see "Behind the Veil," Section 1, below).

Art is closely related to a child's experience of play. Play is gratuitous and free, yet much of play involves learning to find freedom within boundaries. Play involves all the senses. Art is play that pushes the boundaries, even sensory boundaries, forging new rules. As we grow older, these boundaries become more and more prevalent in our lives, and our play becomes more about gaining freedom within rules, such as in sports (we "play" sports) or in music (we "play" music). How can we then continue to play the expanded music of life, the art of life itself as a generative force? What path do we walk to find that "voice" within that can free us from our own diminishment?

What if art can free us to be like a child once again; what if our imagination can be sanctified to see the future hopes as a child of God? What if such an innocent act brings healing to the world, liberating viewers from their confined self-impositions?[3] Of course, such a journey toward the recovery of innocence demands discipline, a discipline committed to developing the art of somatic knowledge.[4]

As William Blake wrote, there are "Songs of Innocence" and "Songs of Experience"; they are both important parts of our generative journey. A mastery of any kind requires a long-term commitment, a vacillation between a recovery of innocence and refining of experience, and regular and constant practice. Just as a sado practitioner can practice sado for more than fifteen years and still not achieve mastery, but only increased humility, any form of expression that connects the body and the mind will require a long-term journey. In that somatic liturgy we integrate all the separations that the mind has created.

It is hard to play as a child without the healthy dependence on and trust in the world. I suppose that even children who are in war zones today find some way to play, but eventually that trust is stolen from them, turning them into child soldiers. We are in war zones of culture wars that can turn all of us into soldiers. We all need a stone path to our studios, to slow down, in our frenzied war zones of trauma.

Navigating between Experience and Innocence, we encounter an interesting portal, a place where these paradoxes are held together. It is a portal where dependence on materiality leads to transcendence through mastery. Those who cross the threshold, like the wardrobe into Narnia, will change how they live on this side of eternity, knowing the world of abundance and delight beyond the portal. Nihonga colors are prismatic, layers of care in a fractured culture. But so much can get in the way, as our hearts are full of distractions, weeds for our attention.

Weeding

In the ritual of walking the path toward the studio, I often pause, bend to take a weed out of the sandy patches in between the stones. A Zen priest told me with disdain once, "Weeds can somehow pop up the moment you turn away."

After being a caretaker of a patch of land, I now have come to know deeply what he meant.

I have been learning from dandelions, though. I used to despise them, in the same tone that the Zen priest spoke of weeds. A friend, a writer, challenged me when she was visiting: "Why do you so dislike dandelions?" Since then, I have been diligent in learning about them, to "love my enemies." I have learned of the remarkable benefit that dandelion tea and dandelion leaves are to our bodies, and how their resilience is gratuitously and freely given to us. Writer Clare Coffey recently wrote, in the appropriately titled "Dandelions: An

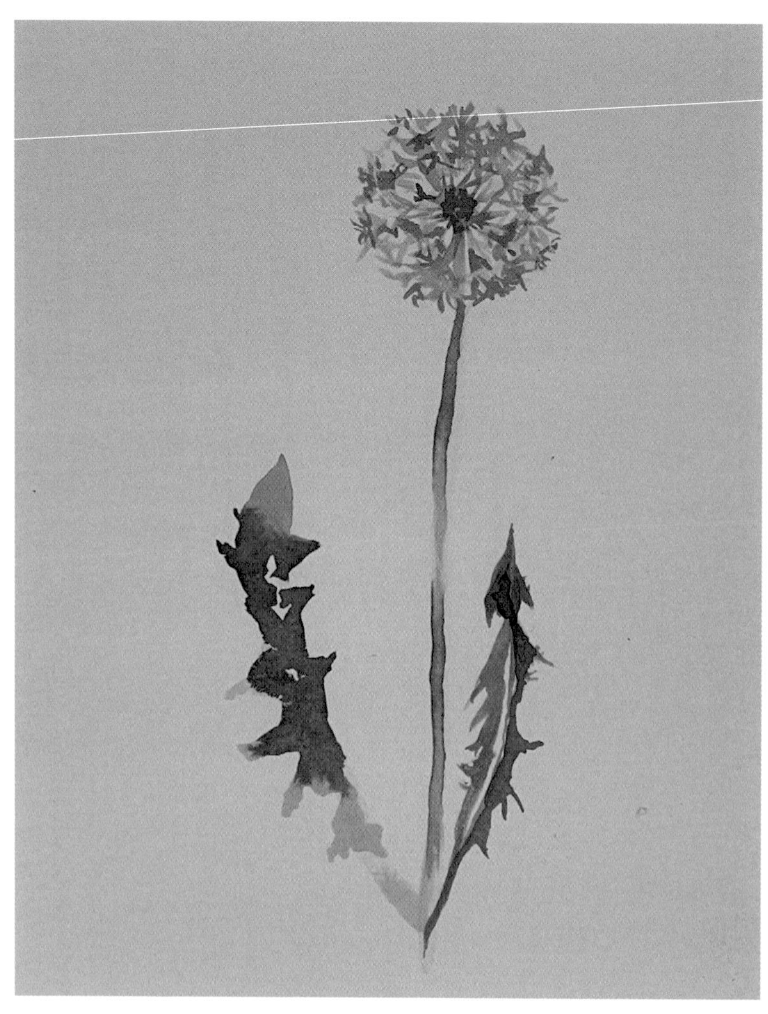

"Dandelion" illustration, 2024, sumi ink on paper.
Copyright © 2024 Makoto Fujimura.

Apology," of Lilias Trotter, a nineteenth-century British artist. Coffey quoted Trotter writing about dandelions, which untangled me from my disdain:

> The dandelion has long ago surrendered its golden petals, and has reached its crowning stage of dying—the delicate seed-globe must break up now—it gives till it has nothing left.
>
> What a revolution would come over the world—the world of starving bodies at home, the world of starving souls abroad—if something like this were the standard of giving; if God's people ventured on "making themselves poor" as Jesus did, for the sake of the need around . . .
>
> The hour of this new dying is clearly defined to the dandelion globe; it is marked by detachment. There is no sense of wrenching; it stands ready, holding up its little life, not knowing when or where or how the wind that bloweth where it listeth may carry it away.

COFFEY CONCLUDES, "The dandelion is an obvious sign of the love of Christ: as Trotter notes, for its uncalculating, diffusive self-emptying."[5] Coffey identifies Trotter as a "missionary, writer and artist." For someone like Trotter—a disciple of the famed John Ruskin, but instead of pursuing a career as a painter, she chose to journey into impoverished Algeria—such labels are appropriate descriptors. As I struggle with easy labels, I think that Trotter should always be regarded as simply an artist whose life was drawn out into the path of the margins, and that her life, as an artwork of God, needs to not be seen as an anomaly. What is seen as strange and extraordinary is what gives essential core to our being. Art is a path toward loving what we disdain, even if that is a label the world puts upon us, and even if the label you placed on yourself is delimiting. What is authentic may belie what is inside of us, but we may not find it until we face what we have tried to kill, exclude, destroy, and weed out in our own hearts. We may yet become lovely by loving what we disdain.

I could not see what Trotter saw in scattering dandelion seeds, this purity of self-giving. Trotter, as well as my writer friend, calls me into metanoia, a turning around of minds and hearts, to be untangled in our obsession to despise, giving loving attention to even what is dismissed, and to those seen as unbeautiful. Perhaps, in giving away such a generative vision, Trotter should be regarded as one of the great artists of her generation.

Once, my wife and I were stranded in Quebec after our flight was canceled because of heavy summer storms. We improvised to stay in a motel by the side of a busy highway. I had to walk about a mile on a narrow path along the road to buy water and essentials. On the way, I passed by many day workers and mothers with strollers and locals who used the path to get to work and home. The road was dusty, with much construction along the way, and did not feel very safe.

On the side of the walkway, weeds grew, with, of course, dandelions, but also blue and yellow flowers I did not recognize. I stopped to consider them.[6] I later found out that the blue flowers were common chicory (*Cichorium intybus*), a cousin of dandelions. I thought about that city, with harsh winter winds and snows that envelop its streets, and day workers and mothers who nonetheless have to walk along that path to get to work or to buy groceries. Snow no doubt accumulates quickly on some days, and the side of the highway will be a mountain of snow mixed with salt.

It took a certain outsized resilience to be a weed there. And in between fumes of buses and trucks, those tall weeds grew, seeking the sun and still flowering and generating beauty. That drawn path of resilience, I reckoned, is what we need now in the world. Perhaps art, like weeds, continues to grow despite the harshness of cultural winds; perhaps art can reflect the ordinary margins of everyday workers, refracting their dignity in their journeys. I imagined that native peoples of the area trod their tribal paths toward the riverbeds, now fully covered by concrete highways, as well as Chinese railroad workers whose descendants now meander upon those sidewalks. Deep in the soil under modern pavements are histories and lives of native tribes and families displaced and submerged in our expediencies. When I stopped by the only place locally that seemed to have coffee, a McDonald's across the barriers of highways, I noticed that one of the locals had created an improvised stone path, right beneath the red post of the McDonald's sign, a stone path much like the one that leads to my studio, except this path was made with fragments of broken-up concrete, on a corner of a grass hill so that the walkers did not have to use the dangerous car lanes.

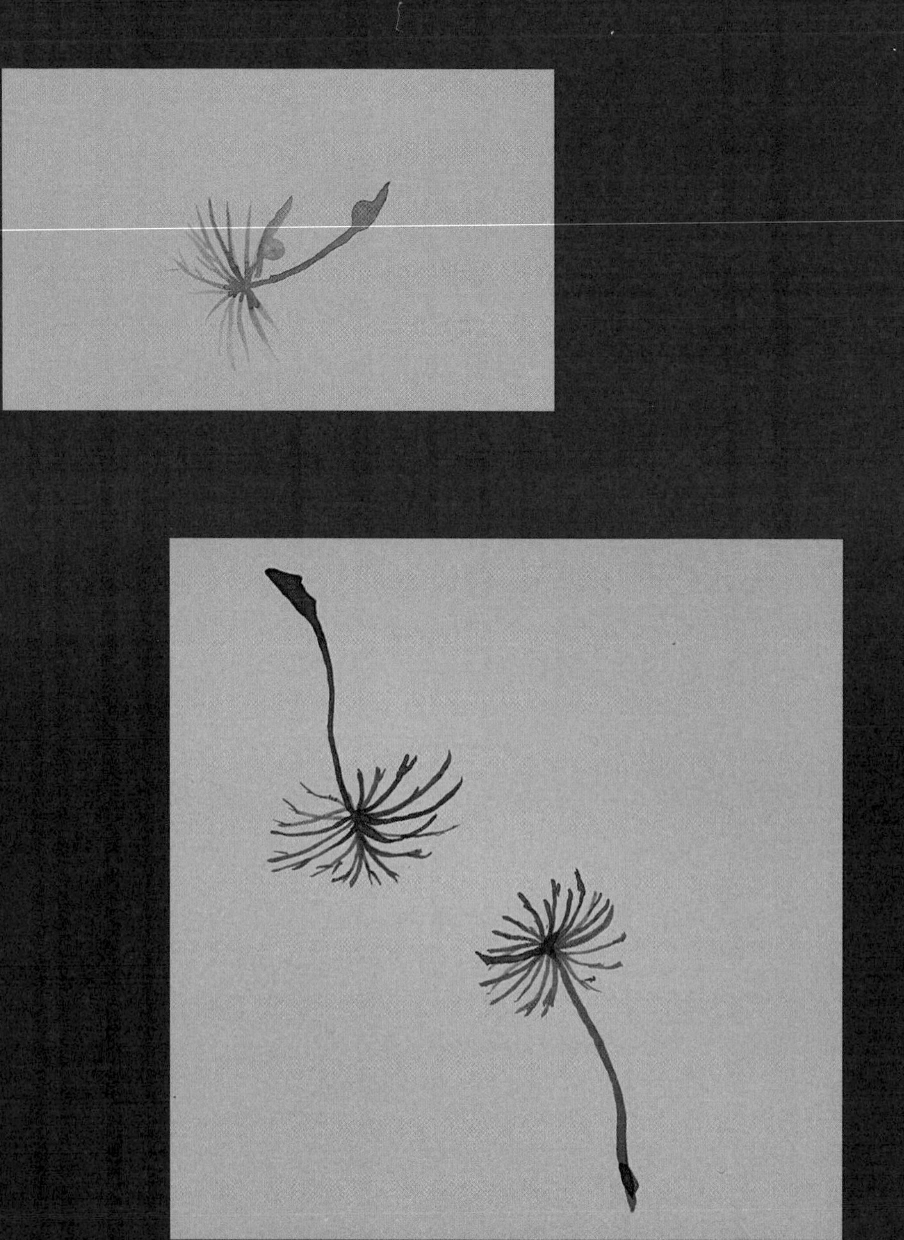

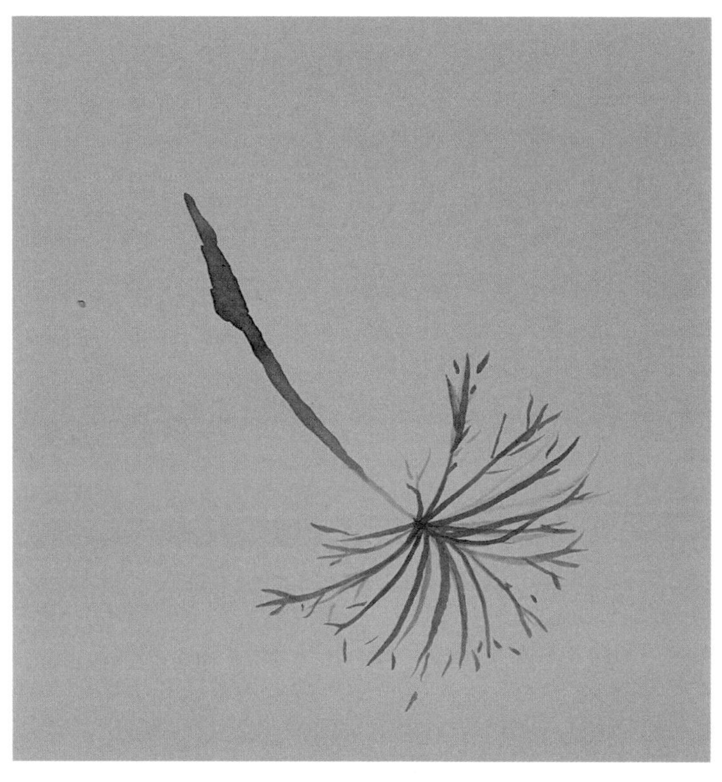

"Dandelion Seeds" illustrations, 2024, sumi ink on paper. Copyright © 2024 Makoto Fujimura.

I stepped on those fragments of stones, balancing my coffee and groceries, grateful for the kindness of those who live and work in the margins.

Art is the hard work of considering the weeds, editing and curating, digging out the deep-rooted hubris of making a name for ourselves and our art. If you create art to be noticed, that art can grow only shallow roots, and you will not develop the resilience of hope through a harsh winter of dismissals and rejection letters. It is in the habit of giving away beauty, of developing, through many failures, a resilient humility, that art can grow to serve rather than to be served. The word *kenosis*—"self-giving"—captures this kind of weeding process well: "it gives till it has nothing left."

The only path toward a new expression is through years of genuine struggle and dying to self. Ironically, the "self" is not found through self-expression but through playing in a prismatic light of what is discarded. The irony is that the art world is made of creating prestige, and the system is set up not to give anything away, but instead to hold on to power. In such a spectacle, the statement "it gives till it has nothing left" may seem like an impossibility. But ones who stayed pure to the call, like Vincent van Gogh, Emily Dickinson, or William Blake, did find themselves prodigiously giving themselves away as dandelion seeds until the end. It's where the seeds land that ultimately starts a new sapling of New Creation.

Prismatic

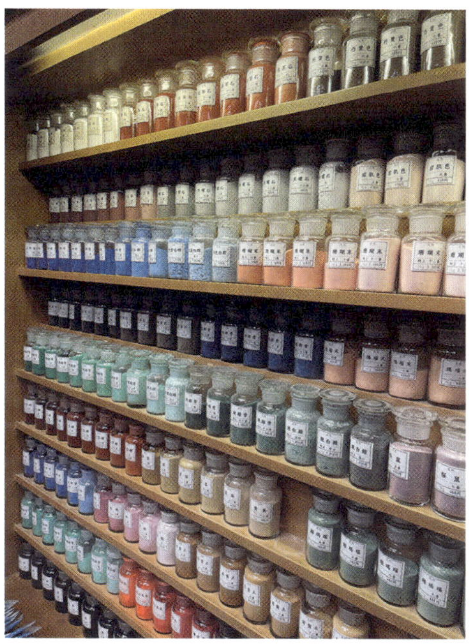

Mineral pigments at the Nihonga supply shop in
Tokyo. Photo credit Makoto Fujimura.

Getting off the commuter train at Ueno Station in Tokyo, I immediately hit a wall of hot and humid air pushing against the cooler fans of the train. Ueno Station seems always crowded, jammed with many visitors to Ueno Park, their energy anticipating their day in one of the key cultural hubs of Tokyo. The National Museum, just beyond the large fountain with rows of pigeons cooing at the edges, and a few other notable museums are nestled together, with a major concert hall often aglow, buzzing after a concert with well-dressed attendees.

In the cherry-lined path, dark viridian now in the summer, vendors line up in rows, with one turning squid basted with soy sauce over coals, and the tangy smoke; another vendor swirls pink threads of cotton candy. With these treats in hand, children wearing straw hats run toward their families headed to the zoo. Tokyo University of the Arts sits beyond the park, at the edge of the newly built museums. Beyond the university lie the sleepy old streets of Shitamachi (the "lower city" or "old city," hearkening back to the seventeenth- to mid-eighteenth-century Edo period).

I rush past the congested rotunda, already perspiring from the summer sun, my feet naturally aligned toward the shady side of Ueno side streets of the old city. The cicadas sing in syncopation, their choral rings echoing in the walled-in narrow streets. Beyond the red-brick walls are the studios where I spent my days at Tokyo University of the Arts. I often took this narrow path away from congestion to the calm of the old city, in between painting the gestural surface of a work drying, somewhat exhausted from the day's work, pushing the limits of my work upon the linoleum-covered concrete floors of the student studios. I looked forward to my walk, as I regularly headed to a venerable Nihonga supply shop, with its jars of resplendent minerals, in the narrow labyrinth of old Tokyo.

The glass door opens slowly, and I wait for the cool air to envelop my face, welcoming me as I step into the Nihonga supply shop. In the small, narrow store filled with extravagantly colored minerals, I am always greeted by Ms. M, the shop owner, who has known me for more than thirty-five years. She remembers me as a student, curious about all things that her grandfather would speak of. Her grandfather once invited me in, to answer all my questions, offering me *somen,* a thin rice noodle served cold in ice water. More than my questions, I remember the aroma of the *dashi* dipping sauce and cold noodles slipping down my throat, sensing the past generational stewardship of Nihonga materials, and satiating my midday hunger. At the time, I remember, I was fasting from lunch, trying to save up to purchase the best gold sheets that I could buy.

When Ms. M measures the minerals, she still uses the antique manual scales that her grandfather used. The minerals are placed on wax paper that is used for measuring medicine. To me, *iwa-enogu* (mineral pigments) are still medicines of beauty, hand-folded in wax paper with care, gem sands cascading into the plastic bag for fifteen grams of delight, and slow art. Flowing sands of elegance replace, for a moment, the tech-frenzied world of digital images.

Now, back in my studio in Princeton, I feel the subtle somatic cues in the tips of my fingers as I mix the unique batch of azurite, particularized for my use by the care of Nihonga shop owners, mixing them with the Nikawa glue in white porcelain, pouring out what has been carefully prepared for me. Like a child walking on the Kamakura beach, I allow the flow of water to gently caress my fingers, a playful mixing that leads to my journey into the light.

Blueberry

Once, during the coronavirus pandemic, Ms. M sent me a sample she thought I might like. In a note she wrote: "I thought you would like this unique color. I thought of you when I saw this batch. Let us know if you want more." Every now and then, I am reminded that I am connected, halfway around the world, by caring thoughts to a Nihonga ecosystem. Every now and then, I see a glimpse of how commerce could be, how it used to be, or how it ought to be.

The sample turned out to be a rather unusual, and limited, amount of azurite, most likely from the edges of copper mines where dynamite chars the azurite. Usually, these charred bits are not excavated but are thrown out to get at the copper. But these "smoky" remains captured my imagination. This was at the end of the pandemic shutdown. The color felt "right" to me as an emblem of our times, as an elegy of the pandemic that caused the loss of so many lives and continues to affect our health journeys.

I asked her to send all that she had.

The azurite became a series of meditations called the *Blueberry* series, perhaps my way of responding to the pandemic silence and darkness. It is painted only with this unique azurite and Nikawa. Artists painting on linen usually prepare it with rabbit skin glue, or more modern gesso, an acrylic alternative, in order to stabilize and create a smooth surface for the pigments going on top. But for this series, I simply wanted one material to go on delicate Belgium linen. There is no substrate underneath to hold the pigments, so at first, the pigments go right through the linen. I capture them in plastic and reuse them. Layers and layers are done in prayer. It takes about thirty layers for the linen to become saturated, and ultimately more than two hundred layers for it to finally start to settle evenly. Then I ask the surface whether it is finished or not.

People ask me, "When do you know whether a work is done?" My answer has always been, "When the work is most pregnant—about to give birth to ten other paintings." *Blueberry* is bursting with possibilities.

Haejin, my bride, came into the studio.[7] She took one look at the first *Blueberry* (then untitled, and not even signed) and said, "We need to create a room for this."

"That will be nice," I said, "but it's not gonna even fit through the door to the farmhouse. We don't have a wall for it either."

It's amazing that the artist can be the one to not think generatively, shutting down an idea before even trying; but my wife, the lawyer, has always pushed me to be an artist.

Haejin was right; the painting did fit through the door. After we moved our furniture around, *Blueberry* hung perfectly on the wall that had been behind one of the couches. I decided then to title it as such, as we can see blueberry bushes from the window that faces the farmland. The surface looked like what a blueberry looks like frosted with morning dew.

Blueberry, 2022, mineral pigments on Belgium linen, 64 × 80 in.
Copyright © 2022 Makoto Fujimura.

The Morning Dew

The room gets morning light from the east window, and I trace the light in the morning, taking multiple photos to post them online.[8] An art curator came to the farm from Japan and sat in front of this work while we planned an exhibit. After we were done speaking about another piece that would be in the exhibit, he said, "I want this work to be in our museum exhibit as well." He thought that the work fulfilled what Mark Rothko began to express even in his last days. *Blueberry* doesn't just capture light; it emanates light from within. The "monochromatic" surface shimmers because of highly pulverized pigments, especially in shifting morning light, to dance with exuberance and joy. Or it can be silent and elusive, closed and open, a "mirror," as my daughter said once, pondering the surface, reflecting what we need to see in it.

We placed the playful gestural painting, painted when I was three years old, next to it. Together, the paintings span some sixty years of time, but to me they are the same, contiguous painting.[9]

Chapter 5

Slow Art

A Cross-Cultural Navigation

In Japanese, my name is written in katakana, a phonetic alphabet that designates a foreign object like "piano" or "sandwich." This way of writing my name is proof of my outsider status. I can never be truly an insider in Japan, an isolationist culture, even if I speak and write in fluent Japanese. In America, I am also thought of as a foreigner, and many good-hearted Americans ask me, "Where are you from?," expecting me to name a country in Asia. I answer, "I was born in Boston, then lived in Sweden, and went to grade school in Kamakura, Japan."

In my journey navigating back to America in my early teens and then traversing between the East and the West as an adult, art has helped me circumnavigate the gaps, and I have developed a keen sense of both cultures. When I am in America, I am highly sensitive to my heart's longing to understand Japanese culture more deeply. When I live for some time in Japan, American culture becomes clearer to me. I've assimilated the value of individualism, and the expressions birthed by some of the most indelible art of the twentieth century. Navigating between Rikyū and Rothko, for instance, I have found that the "gaps" I assumed seem less pronounced. I found also that the Japanese way of seeing the world already inhabits the minds of New York artists, and younger generations of anime lovers, even if they themselves are not quite aware of that or are not ready to admit it. But because I am exiled even from the culture of my roots, that liminal space is helpful for me to see clearly the values of Japanese culture, values that even the Japanese may not be aware of. Of all the Japanese graduate students I shared my master's level class with, I was, by far, most interested in Rikyū.

But ultimately, my art of vacillation in between has become a portal, a portal into a new journey of blended identities, exilic consciousness, and appreciation for all cultures. Such "border-stalking" journeys of an artist can help all of us to understand the liminal spaces between life and death, the mysteries of the unknown.[1] For such a journey we need to take together a slow walk into art.

Rest

Art cannot be seen fully until our minds, usually filled with fears and anxiety, are given rest. Beauty cannot be embraced until we lay down our swords, just like a samurai entering a teahouse in humility and trust, and entrust ourselves to the slowness of being fully present in a tea ceremony, a liturgy of peace. Art is a liturgy of peace. Fear and anxiety can lead to destructive paths, ones driven by our survival mechanisms. Beauty, true beauty, is a longer path for peace, com-

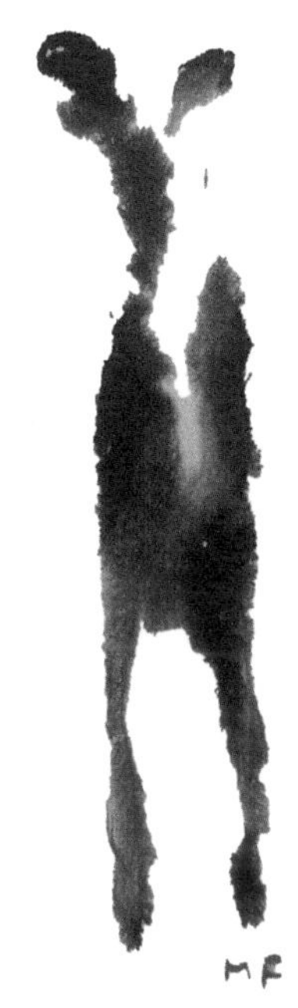

"Deer" illustration, 2024,
sumi ink on paper.
Copyright © 2024
Makoto Fujimura.

munion, and love. We need a rhythm of making that creates a path of abundant care in beauty during uncertain times.

My friend Jordan Kassalow, a renowned eye doctor, told me recently: "If we are relaxed, the lens of our eye and pupil change such that we experience dilated vision, we see in panoramic vision. When we are stressed or excited the optics of our eye changes such that the aperture of our experience shrinks, and we get a narrow or constricted view of the world."[2]

I was explaining to him that I tend to see in "panorama" mode, noting the details from the peripheral view and not simply seeing things in front of me. Apparently, I am experiencing the world in "dilated vision," even when I see weeds or am drawn to colors like hummingbirds.

When I paint, it seems that I also have developed a "liturgy" of sorts, perhaps to navigate the labyrinth of complex and peripheral sensory experiences as I journey in and out of my sacred space and the process of "slow art." The walk from my house to the barn is less than a minute. But as I have described, in that short span, so much information flows through my eyes, which filter the details unconsciously, as seeds for my intuition to grow. I need, then, a way to tend the soil of my observations, so that I can integrate a kaleidoscope of details and flow on the surface of my paintings.

One observer, watching me prepare myself to paint, likened the motion of my hands to those of a seasoned baseball player getting ready to bat. Years of preparation and repeating a task with diligent attention creates an unconscious rhythm. The word "liturgy" denotes a seasonal rhythm to religious calendars, but we all have a form of liturgy, whether it be what we do to prepare for our days at work, how we root for a sports team, or the nine-to-five rhythms of work. This book is a way to capture that liturgical rhythm of making with words, an invitation to how I journey into my creative acts, what I see in a world full of burning bushes, and a way to see deeply the light that is already at hand. The liturgy of making opens our sensory perceptions and cultivates our somatic knowledge. This liturgy will give us peace.

David Brooks of the *New York Times* wrote about his experience at one of my exhibits: "Nihonga is slow to make and slow to see. Mako once advised me to stare at one of his paintings for 10 to 12 minutes. I thought it would be boring, but it was astonishing. As I stood still in front of it, my eyes adjusted to the work. What had seemed like a plain blue field now looked like a galaxy of color."[3]

A blue field becoming a galaxy of color. Art can help us to get there, from an anxiety-driven world to a galaxy of color that our eyes were created to see, especially in the dimness of our late days. No matter whether we are artists or journalists, engineers or plumbers, shepherds or kings, we can see the "galaxy of color" embedded in the pulverized world all around us.

Again, there is a difference between seeing *with* the eye and seeing *through* the eye. What is that difference? Someday, machine technology will perhaps simulate seeing *with* the eye. But seeing *through* the eye is to envision the essence of our being, to "see" the future states within and through reality in front of us. Every enduring artwork, in some ways, captures the future orientation of the world that is becoming. Every work that captures truth sees *through* the mask we wear, and façade of walls that limits us to our scarcity mindset of zero-sum gain, into a world of reality breaking into our lives every moment. Therefore, no matter how powerful the machine language of "A.I." pattern making can become, one that we see in social media platforms now, it will not train us to see *through* the eye, to generatively create beyond the digital fragments. We need to consider a cross-cultural journey to discover what it means to see *through* the eye and apply that to our local conditions.

Walking on Water

On March 11, 2011, I was in my studio working in New York City when I began to hear cries for help in my social media feeds. Strangers in northern Japan were asking for help locating relatives missing from Ishinomaki after the great Tohoku earthquake and tsunami of that day. Ishinomaki is an area I know well, as that seascape is connected to a masterpiece by the seventeenth-century artist Tawaraya Sotatsu that now is known as *Waves at Matsushima* and is in collection at the National Museum of Asian Art in Washington, DC. Matsushima, as an emblem of the power of nature, was painted by many masters over and over as an icon of Japanese aesthetic and the threshold of nature's power breaking into their imagination, and to test their skill. As we will see, another Matsushima work (at the Museum of Fine Arts in Boston) impacted my young journey as an artist. The materi-

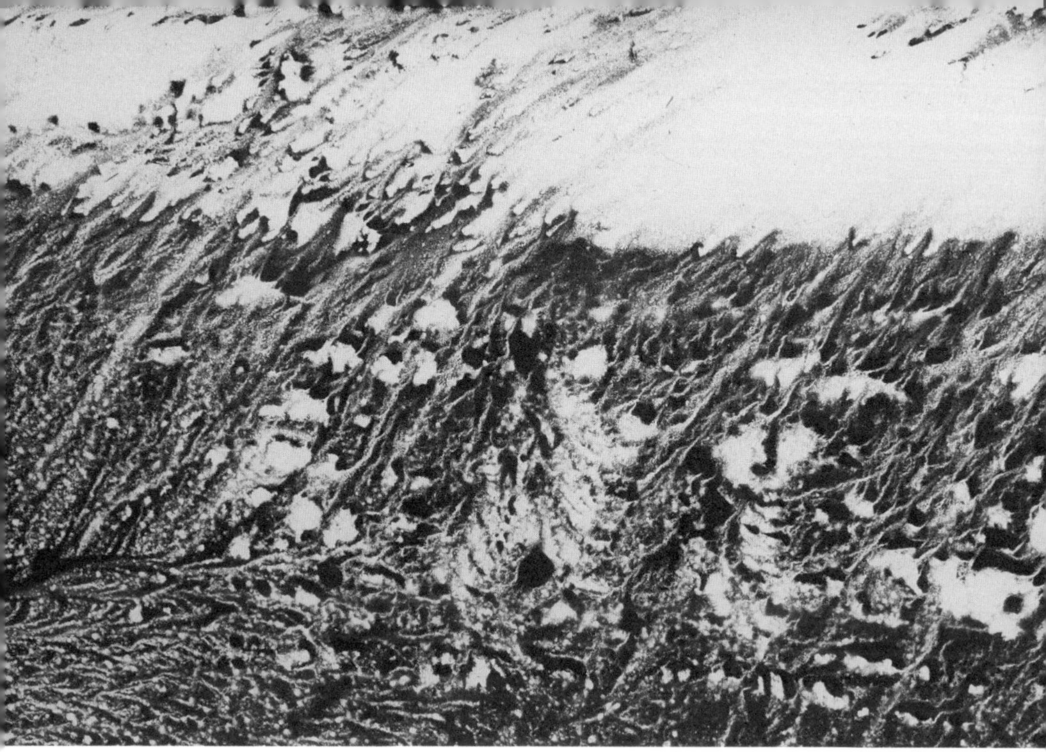

"Sand Patterns," detail from *Walking on Water* series.
Copyright © 2020 Makoto Fujimura.

als used here, malachite, gofun white, gold on paper, are exactly the same materials I use today.

I wept, for the number of lives taken by the earthquake and tsunami was beyond even what earthquake-prone Japan could bear. The tsunami washed away entire fishing villages of generations of Japanese families, leaving many schoolchildren orphaned. The Fukushima Daiichi nuclear power plant was also damaged severely, and the catastrophic reactor core meltdown led to the plant having

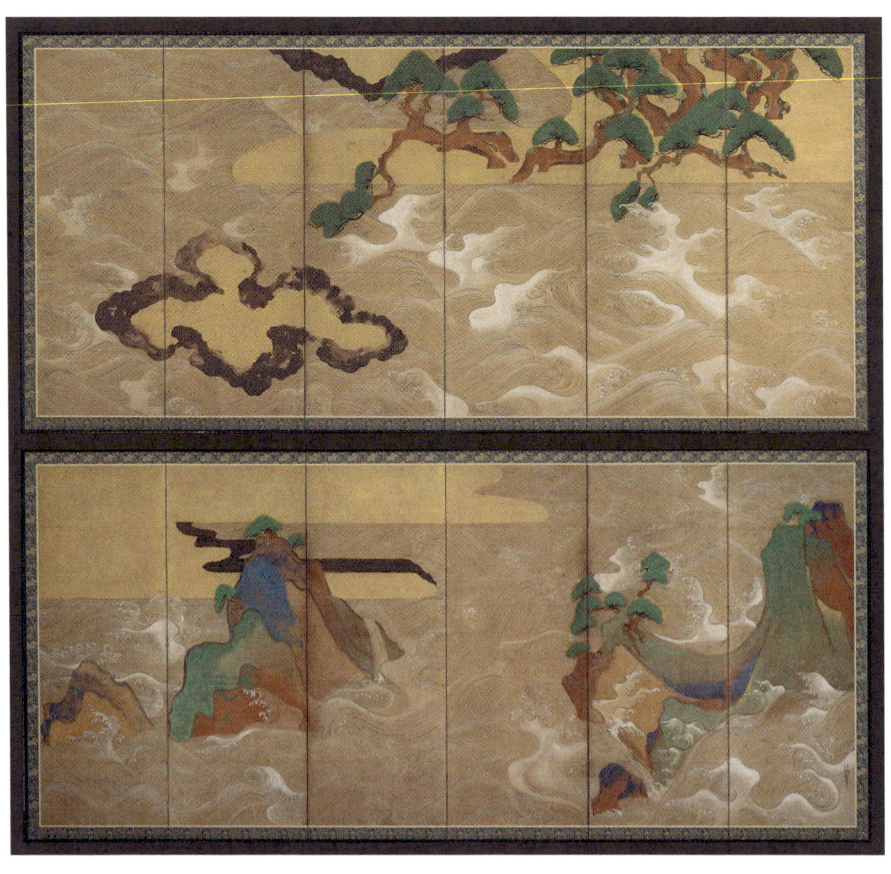

Tawaraya Sotatsu 俵屋宗達 (fl. ca. 1600–1643), *Waves at Matsushima,*
seventeenth-century Japan, ink, color, gold, and silver on paper, each panel 166 ×
369.9 cm. (65 3/8 × 145 5/8 in.). Smithsonian National Museum of Asian Art.

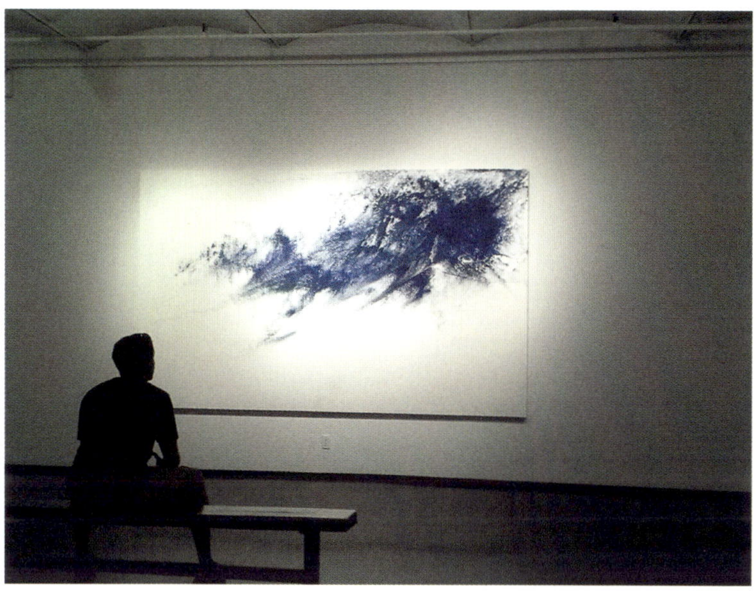

Walking on Water—Azurite, 2012, azurite on canvas with polished gesso,
84 × 132 in. Copyright © 2012 Makoto Fujimura.
Exhibit installation photo credit Makoto Fujimura.

to be shut down. I feared that the Matsushima scene was entirely gone.

I began a series of paintings, as an elegy to the victims of the earthquake and tsunami, called *Walking on Water*, a monumental painting spanning eleven to twelve feet, which continues to this day. The question "Can we walk on water?" has been extended to the climate crisis at large, elegies to all that has been lost. But at the same time the audacity to ask such an impossible question is also generative, invoking hope.

I visited Ishinomaki in April 2011, a month after the earthquake. I shared about this experience in a commencement speech I gave a week later and wrote on the return flight to the United States.[4] In my mind I kept on seeing the upside-down fishing boat on top of the elementary school, where many displaced orphans were staying. The stench of rice fields filled with salt water and the ongoing nuclear power plant crisis still haunt me. The pine-covered island that Sotatsu evoked, which I feared to be lost after the tsunami, survived. I saw, as I ventured to the stench of the Ishinomaki beach, the ravaged pine trees still standing on the misshaped landscape. The landscape has changed forever, making the painting even more valuable.

The painting of Matsushima, too, has had a severe journey of its own and could have been lost in the rapid shift of Japanese culture during the Meiji Restoration and later the World War II bombing of Japan, had it not been for advocates who walked upon the tenuous waters that made two countries into adversaries at war. They worked to bring Japanese culture to America, and to save this treasure and others, as well as the cultural heritage of Japan. Two gentlemen in particular—the Japanese tea connoisseur Okakura Tenshin and his mentor, the Harvard University professor Ernest Fenollosa—who created the very department of Nihonga at Tokyo University of the Arts where I studied.

The Birth of Nihonga

During my time at Bucknell University in Lewisburg, Pennsylvania, as I began to find my calling as an artist, my professors kept on impressing upon me the need to rediscover my heritage and aesthetics. As I wrote earlier, the seminal influence of Kamakura in my aesthetics came out in every painting I attempted to create as a student. One day, my painting professor said, "You need to see firsthand what your heritage means." Being a contrarian, I decided to take a long train ride to Boston to see the famed collection of Japanese paintings at the Museum of Fine Arts there, only to refute my professor's urging and break free of these influences.

When I entered the dark halls to see paintings of the Kano school, I saw works whose lines delineated what I had longed to develop in my work. Even my earliest painting, done when I was three, identified forms and movement that these Japanese masters, such as Ogata Korin, Hasegawa Tohaku, and the Kano school painters, captured elegantly in their works. By the time I returned to Bucknell, my mind had shifted to desiring to study back in Japan. These works beckoned me to my heritage and the culture of Japan. I had not known then of the history of how these works got to US museums, how precarious such a legacy was, and the work of cross-cultural advocacy that saved these poetic lines.

During the Meiji Restoration era (1868–1912), Japan underwent a period of rapid modernization and Westernization after centuries of feudal rule and determined isolationism. The country began to embrace Western cultural influences, causing major societal shifts away from many traditional Japanese artistic practices, to the extent that many of the art forms faced extinction.

Many Japanese artisans and painters who continued their traditional ways found themselves without support. There was a need to delineate and preserve traditional Japanese painting methods and art objects themselves. In 1887, the prominent American art historian and philosopher Ernest Fenollosa, who had lived in Japan for more than a decade to teach at Tokyo Imperial University (later Tokyo University, where my father taught), called for the formal establishment of a system to teach and perpetuate native Japanese painting techniques.

The Nihonga department at Tokyo University of the Arts was formed as a result of his advocacy to preserve Japanese culture. To create a categorical term for traditional painting as opposed to Western-style painting, Fenollosa began to speak of "Japanese painting," which the translator translated as "Nihonga."[5]

During the foaming nationalism and aggression of the Japanese military that would eventually lead to the bombing at Pearl Harbor, Fenollosa, along with other American scholars and patrons, notably Okakura Tenshin (the author of *The Book of Tea* and a student of Fenollosa), Bernard Leach, Charles Lang Freer, and Charles Goddard Weld, worked to preserve Japanese art and indigenous culture by bringing artworks abroad, especially to the United States. They privately shipped many masterworks as their own collections, and many of these ended up in Boston, Philadelphia, Washington, DC,

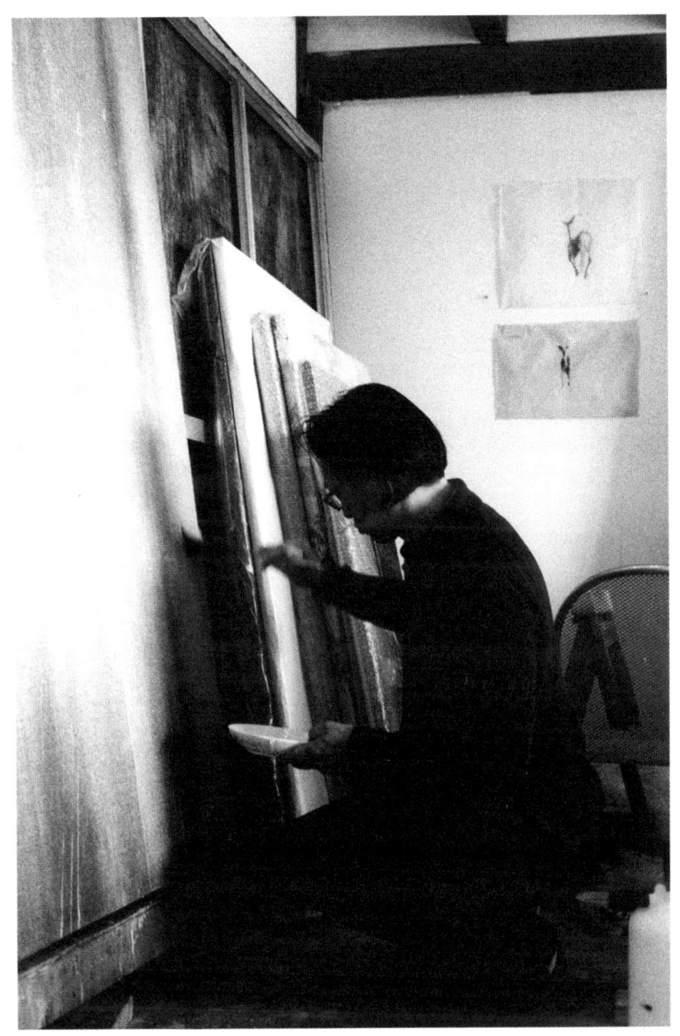

Makoto Fujimura painting *Walking on Water* series.
Photo credit Alyson LeCroy.

and other locations. Because of Fenollosa's personal connection with Weld, he oversaw the establishment of the Japanese art collection at the Museum of Fine Arts in Boston—the collection which had that profound effect on me as a young college student. His early patronage drew me to Nihonga, to Tokyo University of the Arts, and I ended up inheriting this heritage as a rare outsider, becoming accepted into the university's prestigious lineage doctoral program, working out such influence in the contemporary art scene today.

Culture Care

Even in my study of traditional Japanese painting, I became aware that such a legacy does not exist apart from the advocacy provided by outsiders, and the East and West navigations by Japanese counterparts to champion the value of Japanese culture.[6] Fenollosa's efforts laid a foundation for a legacy of advocates for Eastern culture, followed by the contributions of Bernard Leach, Muneyoshi Yanagi, and others. I am able to work out of this legacy today. Thus, to meander in between these cultures is not to be an anomaly in historical terms. Even the term "Nihonga" was coined by an outsider who valued and wanted to protect Japanese heritage.

We are all part of this great convergence of multiple cultural streams, flowing into a fantastically diverse cultural estuary. It is often the "outsiders" who see objectively the lasting value of what "insiders" take for granted. Art flows out of such margins, and artists are border-stalkers of cultural boundaries, reporting back on the very essence of what makes that tribal culture unique. But often, such a journey takes sacrifice, and even the pulverization of the whole.

Rather than seeing Japanese culture as an island culture of homogeneity, we can see it as a "yobi-tsugi" result of mosaic Silk Road cultures before becoming an isolated "island" during the Tokugawa era, and then assimilating and creating something new out of the confluences.[7] Perhaps that refinement is how we, in the West, can learn that out of trauma and violence toward other cultures can still come a culture of resilience. As in yobi-tsugi, we can see in other cultures of fragments a patchwork of hope and dreams. All cultures share that pulverization and trauma—a common curse.[8] That we share in suffering is an invitation to move together into making our yobi-tsugi collectively. Such is the legacy of Sen no Rikyū and many other cultural advocates.

Chapter 6

Pulverized Minerals

As my fingers press and mix the gritty mixture of finely ground minerals used in Nihonga, combining them with the warm Nikawa glue, deep inside the recesses of my cultural memory I am communing with seventeenth-century Japan, a world of Sotatsu and Korin, and the ancient roots of this art form reaching back to the Silk Road. Each coarse grain of azurite, when observed under a microscope, reveals a refractive universe of its own. If the pigments are pulverized by hand by a master artisan, rather than an industrial machine, each pigment, though uniform in weight, has a different shape, with billions of diverse fragments, no two the same.

As William Blake wrote, to see an intricate "World in a Grain of Sand" is to peer into the microstructures that echo the macro expanse of the universe. But to see "a Heaven in a Wild Flower" will require a kind of faith that acknowledges the Creator of that "Heaven." For me, as I had no conviction of what heaven was, these lines seemed like an invitation to another realm of experience. I realized, reading poets like Blake, that my experience of the "flow" is closely connected to the wonderment I sense both in the studio and in nature, and to my growing faith.

ART REFLECTS A COMPLEX JOURNEY of layers and multiple paths, and not a single linear path of chronology. Just like the prismatic light from my pulverized azurite, our faith invites us to not one explanation toward the end, but through multiple entry points, perhaps unique to each one of us, creating a spectrum. Even for me, to experience Blake's "Heaven in a Wild Flower" is to unravel a mystery, many years after my journey of faith began in earnest. The process of pulverization is a way of deconstruction. Our flattened ways of how we think about the world, how we see ourselves, and even how we see God are often one-dimensional, and only through pulverization, our mystery of complexity comes alive.

Thus, minerals must be pulverized first for the layering of prismatic surface to appear. And it seems that our fallen world requires us all to be pulverized as well. The good news is that in that pain is a beautiful mystery. Love's remaining shards, full of even disillusionment and death, can begin to refract in our lives. Our lives are love's remains, prismatic surfaces, shards of mystery, a portal into a greater Reality.

Gravity and Grace

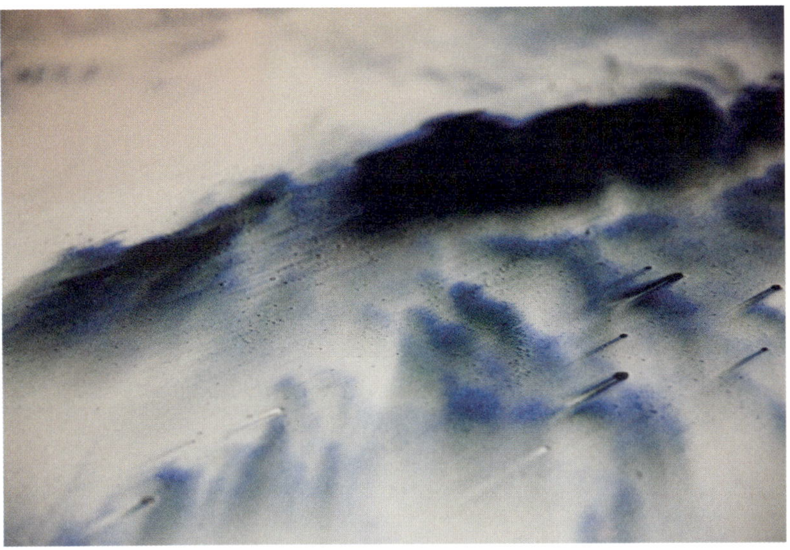

Detail from *Walking on Water* series.
Photo credit Alyson LeCroy. Copyright © Makoto Fujimura.

Simone Weil wrote: "Creation is composed of the descending movement of gravity, the ascending movement of grace and the descending movement of the second degree of grace. Grace is the law of the descending movement."[1]

My art is both gravity and grace. I paint both with panels on the floor and with panels standing up. I let gravity guide the minerals flowing down, but I also create watermarks that are made by

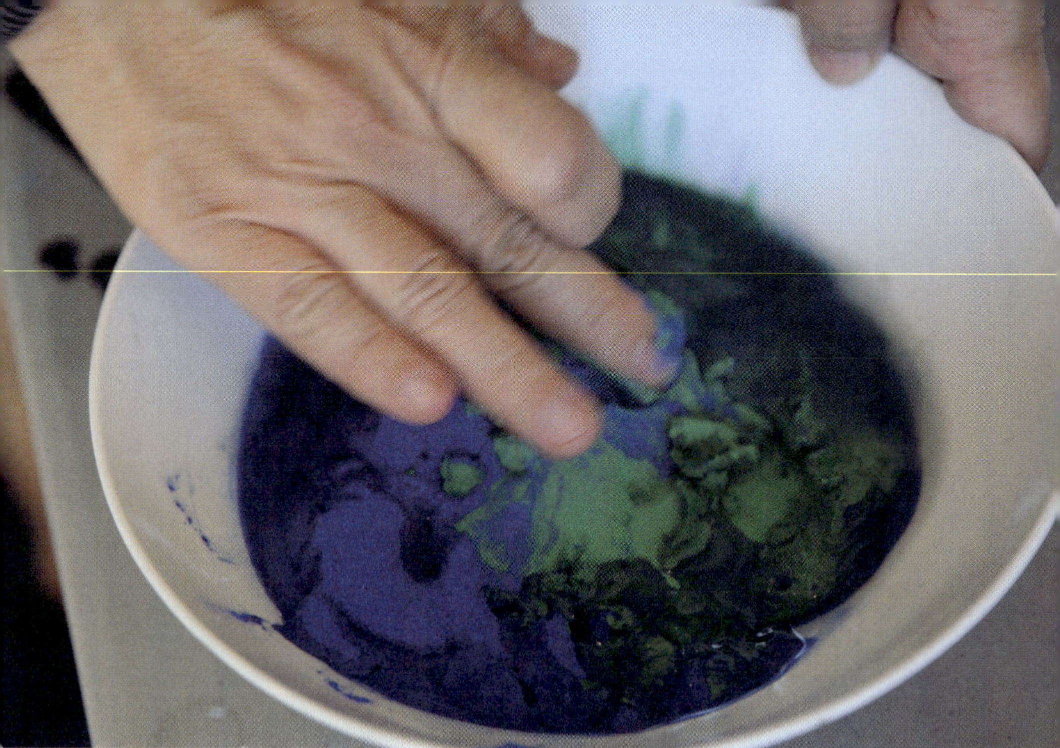

Makoto Fujimura mixing mineral pigments. Photo credit Alyson LeCroy

watching the puddle of water form the watermarks and pouring pigments into them, in the technique of *tarashi-komi* (a technique that Tawaraya Sotatsu is known to have developed). At the same time, I resist gravity, but create images that use the cascading minerals to cause the image to rise. Grace (*charis* in Greek, shortened from *charisma*, gift) permeates in the drips and watermarks, as I ponder my miraculous existence as a survivor of 9/11/2001.

Every day is a gift of *charis*. My trauma on 9/11 made me appreciate each day, each moment I have lived my life as an artist.[2] So many

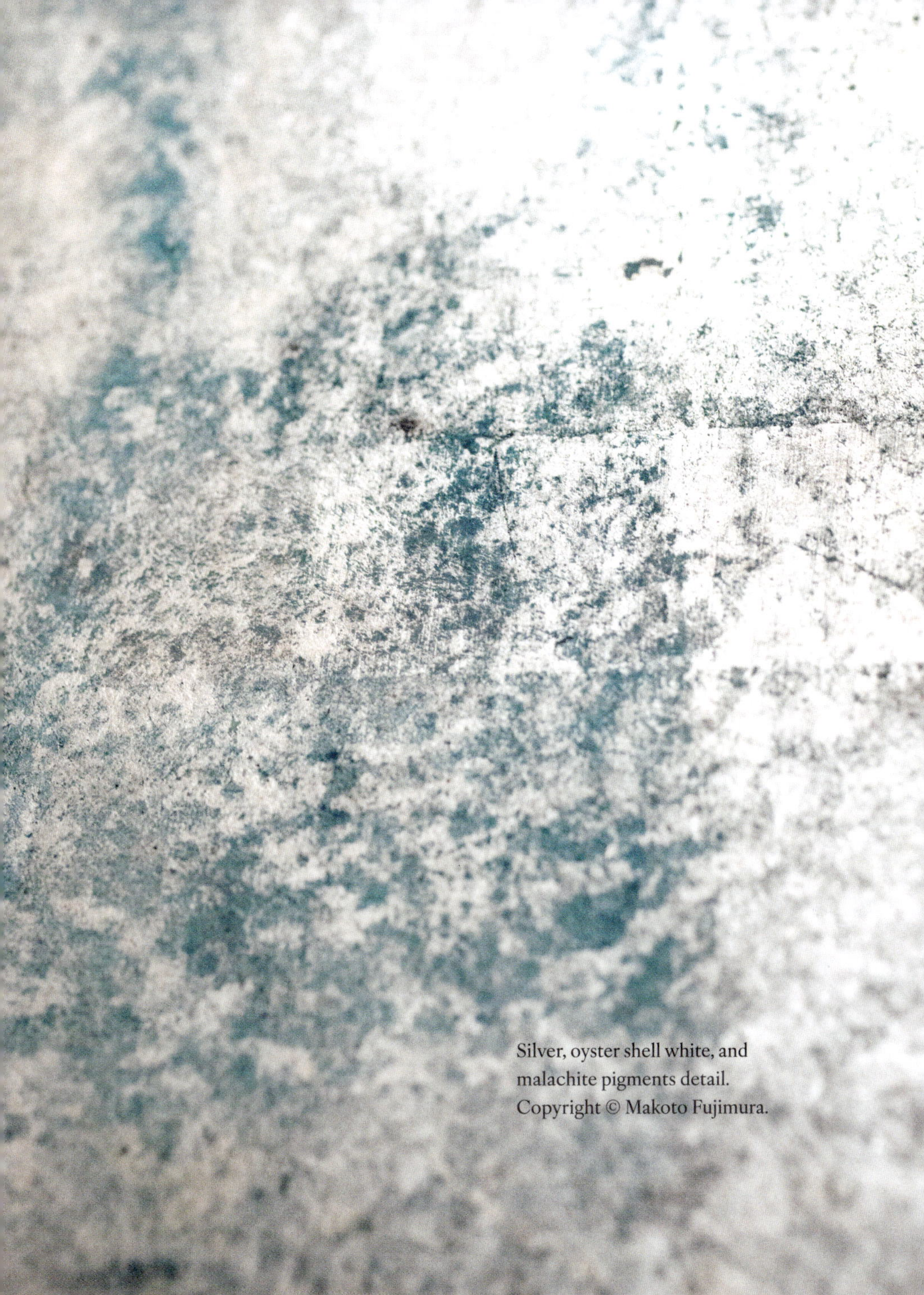

Silver, oyster shell white, and
malachite pigments detail.
Copyright © Makoto Fujimura.

times, I've been told that I have lived an impossible life, that I am a rare phenomenon. Every painting is a witness to that miraculous journey of being alive. I am simply living out a life of following the light of God, the only true Artist. I tell many, "I am the proof that our living God is the Artist, as it is impossible to live the life I have lived if that were not the case." My life may be an enigma to behold, a burning bush, but one that also should be accessible to anyone through faith.

Miracle

My artistic journey made me profoundly aware of how facing the impossible, as living near Ground Zero might force any of us to do, encourages us to constantly face the ashes of destruction in front of us. Artists are always seeking the new, and they often find challenging circumstances to be opportunities. Art creates the future by redefining what the "impossible" is. As Mark Rothko said, "Pictures must be miraculous."[3]

Art questions even what art can be. Art, therefore, is about the impossibility of art. At the same time, artists must be fully present in that realm of impossibility and use their senses to seek beyond that realm. The origin of this possibility, the possibility beyond the "impossible," begins for me by being filled with gratitude that such impossibilities exist at all.

The greatest miracle, the greatest impossibility, is perhaps faith itself. It takes faith to paint, to act onstage, and to write. One might

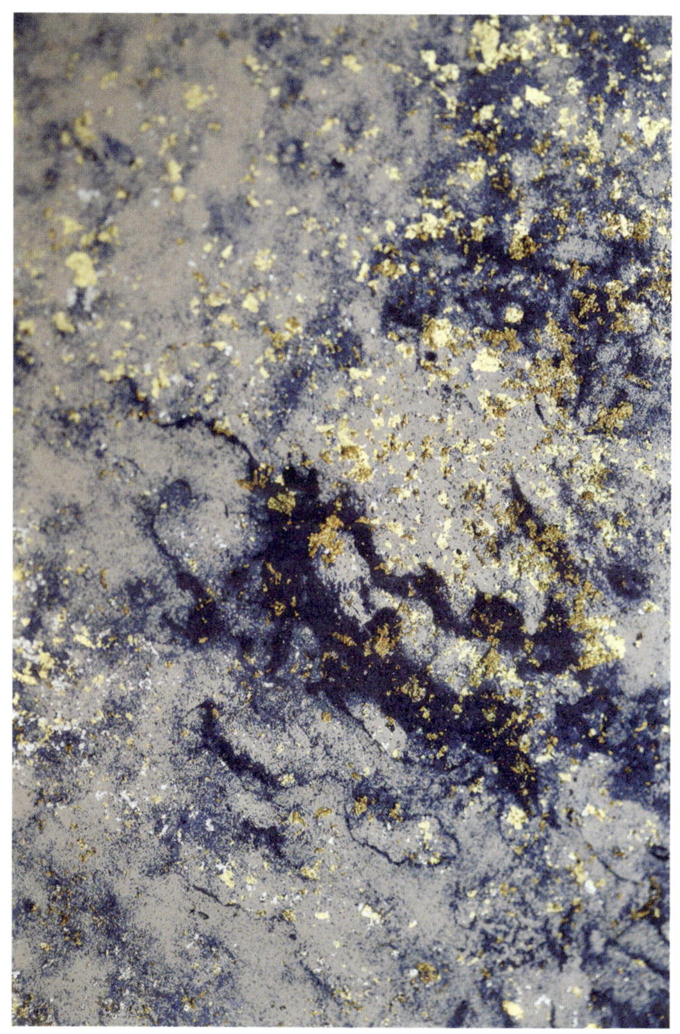

Gold particles detail.
Copyright © Makoto Fujimura.

critique such a broad statement about faith and say that such a faith is not about God, but about faith in art—and warn that with art, humans are creating idols to worship for themselves.

There is a certain danger to making.[4] We all know that we can create a weapon of mass destruction or beautiful paintings. Even a beautiful painting or music can become an idol for us to worship.[5] Through such an idol, we can come to worship our egos, as selfish pride "marches against thee" (see William Blake, "O Lord what can I do: my Selfhood cruel / Marches against thee" below in "Beyond the Veil," Section 1). But such beauty can also free us, to be used to liberate us from our "bondage to decay" into the "glorious freedom of the child of God" (Rom 8:21). For me, such impossibility and quest harken back to the miracle of Easter (see "Beyond the Veil" below).

Such a vacillation between facing impossibilities and dreams does not erase our longings that exist far beneath the reality of making. "Beauty, sooner or later," noted Elaine Scarry, "brings us into contact with our own capacity for making errors."[6] Just like what I experienced in considering the dandelions earlier, such a navigation is full of discoveries of errors and blind spots that lie within.

To create art is to do the "impossible" task of moving beyond survival, moving from a scarcity model to the world of abundance and enduring conversation. Art is not mere self-expression, or a device for finding oneself. Art is prayer. Art is an expression and a response to Love. Love is abundant. Love is generative. Love, again, is a refractive splendor.

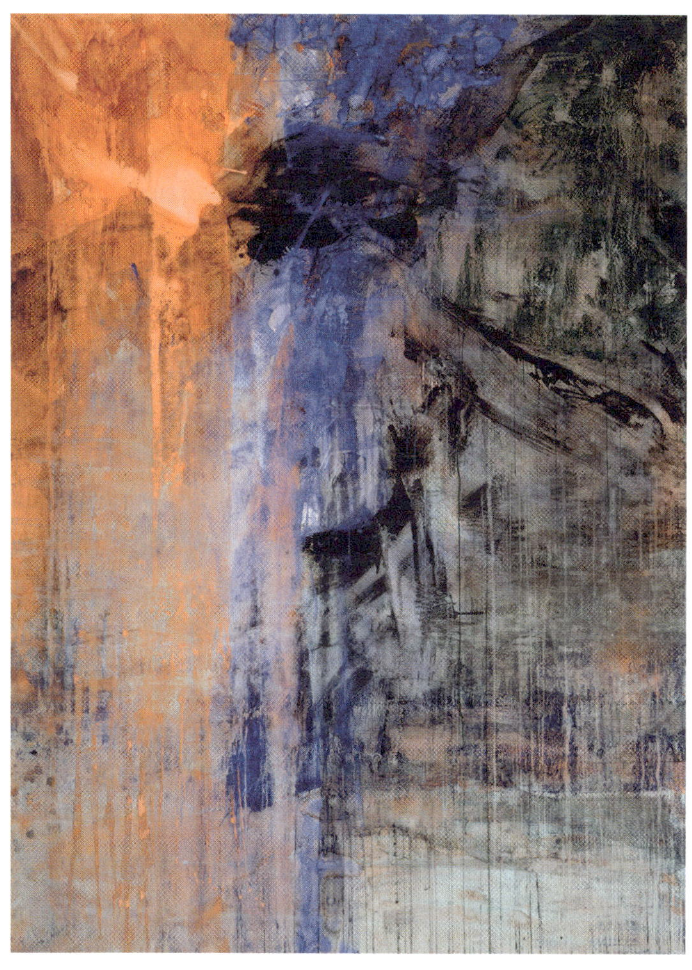

The Fire and the Rose Are One, 2003–2004, mineral pigments on Kumohada paper, 89 × 66 in. Roberta and Howard Ahmanson collection. Copyright © 2004 Makoto Fujimura.

Ground Zero Ashes

I walked on Ground Zero ashes on September 12, 2001, still in a daze. I was trying to get the key documents from our loft three blocks away from where the Twin Towers had stood. I did not know at the time whether our loft would still be standing, as the fire of the fallen towers raged on, with the ground feeling hot to my feet. I waded through about an inch of ashes, the sacred remains of people, as well as the debris of computers, buildings, and Picasso and Miro paintings, which were on exhibition in the Cantor Fitzgerald offices of the North Tower. All incinerated. Seagulls covered the skies, and until that morning I had never thought of seagulls as menacing scavengers of our lives' remains.

I stood facing Ground Zero for many months after that, pondering the soil of ashes. For me, to wake up every morning was literally to face Ground Zero. To come home every day was to face Ground Zero. This unavoidable daily pilgrimage forced in me a discipline of remembrance, and even a kind of repentance.

What is soil? Soil is composed of death and life. Things die and become earth again. But the remarkable thing is that in compost life is once again birthed into another life. If this interaction of life and death does not happen regularly, life will not be as abundant. Ground Zero ashes are composed of the soil of our enmities and loves, now a waterfall of re-membrance, built into the negative spaces of the imprints of the towers.

I began to paint a series of elegiac paintings called *Water Flames*

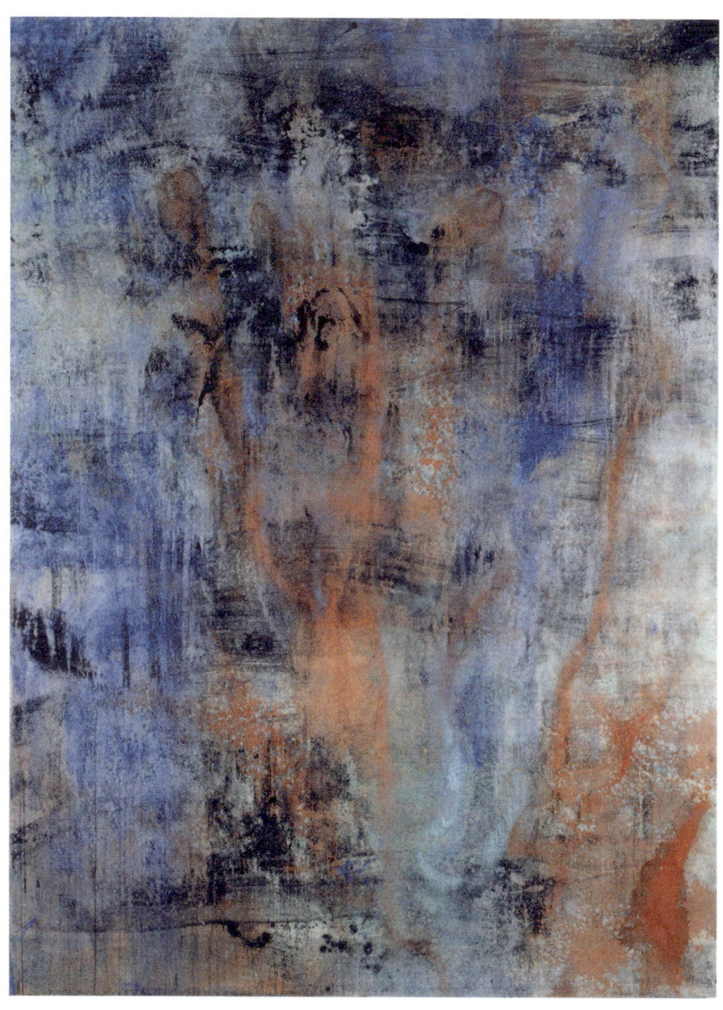

Splendor—Ghost, 2004, mineral pigments on Kumohada paper, 89 × 66 in.
Ty, Clayton, and Lydia Fujimura collection.
Copyright © 2004 Makoto Fujimura.

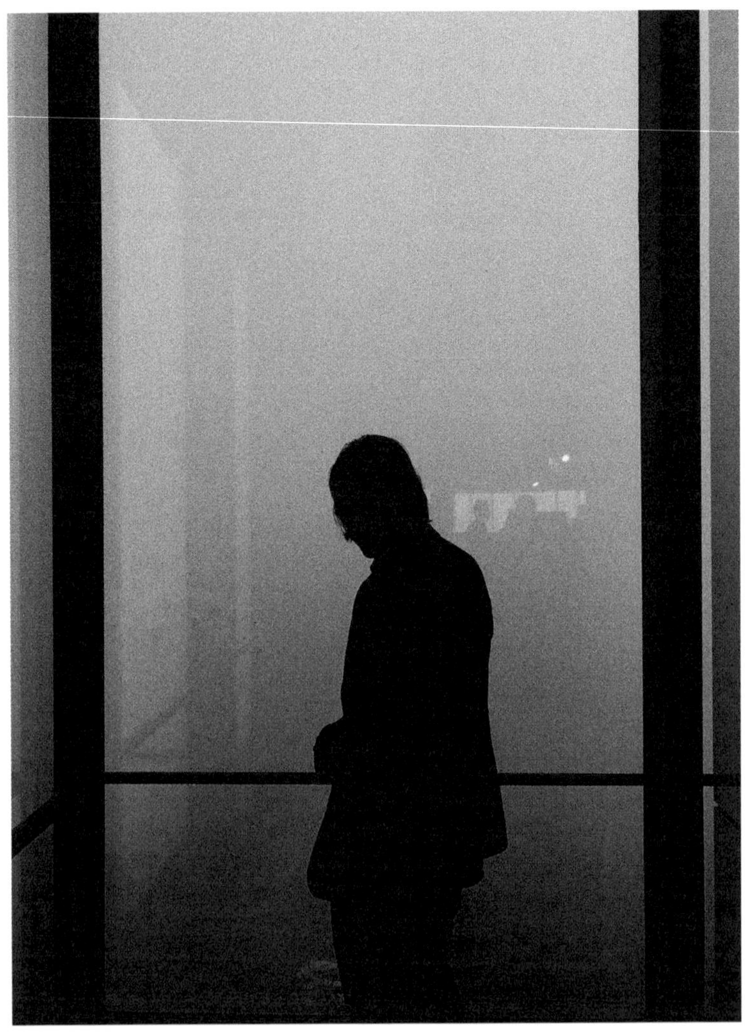

Makoto Fujimura in the at-the-time still unfinished 3 World Trade Center, 2018. Photo by Jeremy Cowart.

soon after. I needed to deal with the ashes, fire, and smoke that pervaded my imagination, haunting my soul. I needed a place to house these specters, and express them, as I did my best to hide my own trauma of that day from my family and grieving friends. Art became my only place to find a path, my Ground Zero studio a refuge, and faith also became a "substance of things hoped for" (Heb 11:1 KJV).

In my studio, I could process pain and fear, and I could express them and be honest about my utter resignation, my feeble prayers. I remember painting these *Water Flames* paintings, how layering over and over became a prayer. My body prayed as I painted, and somehow my spirit returned to my body in the days of trauma and severe darkness to follow. It was a lonely journey of pain.[7] Is my faith a "substance [*hypostasis*] of things hoped for," or is it a substance of trauma? Art is a path to explore this tension, and the "substance," or *hypostasis*, suggests a rich web of generative connections that binds, as the word suggests the power of the invisible strands of resilience, spread all over us, the world, and the cosmos. Hypostasis leads us to the Easter morning of resurrection lives. Hypostasis leads us to all art.

Pain-ting

My *Water Flames* series became the first series of paintings after 9/11. Over and over, I layered minerals on stretched *Kumohada* paper, a paper made by a master papermaker who had passed away several years before. I had kept several rolls of large papers (the largest hand-lifted paper in the world at the time they were made) since his pass-

Water Flames—Doe of the Dawn (Psalm 22), 2021, mineral pigments, Japanese vermillion, gold, platinum powders, and cochineal on canvas, 60 × 96 in. (diptych). "Doe of the Dawn" is one of the heading titles attributed to Psalm 22, a psalm that famously begins with Jesus's words on the cross, "My God, my God, why have you forsaken me?" This diptych was specifically created for the twentieth commemoration of the 9/11 terrorist attacks, for the "Re-membrance" exhibit. Copyright © 2021 Makoto Fujimura.

ing, knowing that the quality of his papers is likely not to be reached again. I continue to paint these images in my studio, often now in modified form on uniquely treated canvas, such as *Water Flames— Doe of the Dawn,* done for the twentieth commemoration of 9/11.

Living at Ground Zero back then, I did not know what the future would hold or even what the painting would become. I was not painting for an exhibit, but only to face the painting, and pain, every day. A poet friend told me then that "painting is pain-ting." Then one day, after spraying the surface with water after several layers of minerals, I noticed that the paper buckled and began to create watermarks. I could have taken the marks out while drying, but I decided to let them form. The next day, I came back to the studio and saw, lying on the ground, an image of flames. Watermarks on Kumohada paper naturally form flames.

As I continued to paint flames with water, I began to intentionally see the flames as potentially sanctifying, and not just destructive. I was recalling the visual language of the apocalyptic, moody paintings of Mark Rothko—but using Japanese vermillion, gold, platinum powders, and cochineal (made from an insect) instead of Magna paint, as Rothko had done. I began to overlay biblical narratives of sanctifying flames.[8]

The recent Japanese paper does not have the same quality that it once had under the last remaining master. Since my layers are so dependent on the consistency of the weaving of the large paper's lifting fibers, I no longer can paint the kind of images I was creating in the mid-2000s. But I find this predicament to be oddly appropriate.

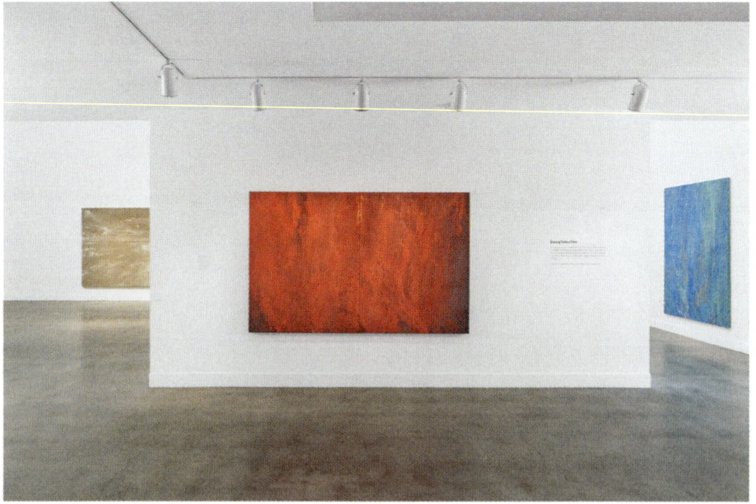

Installation view of *Makoto Fujimura: Water Flames,* Frederick R. Weisman Museum of Art at Pepperdine University, January 13–March 31, 2024. Image courtesy of Frederick R. Weisman Museum of Art. Photo: Angel Xotlanihua.

Flames cause a world to disappear, and water may find resurrection in the ashes.

Mystery

In the fall of 2001, I took a walk to P.S. 234 where my children attended (a public school in Tribeca, near Ground Zero) on the way to my studio, ten blocks north, and took a turn, around the corner from my loft. It was an unusually cold day for November, and I noticed a little commotion in the maple tree. This was one of the

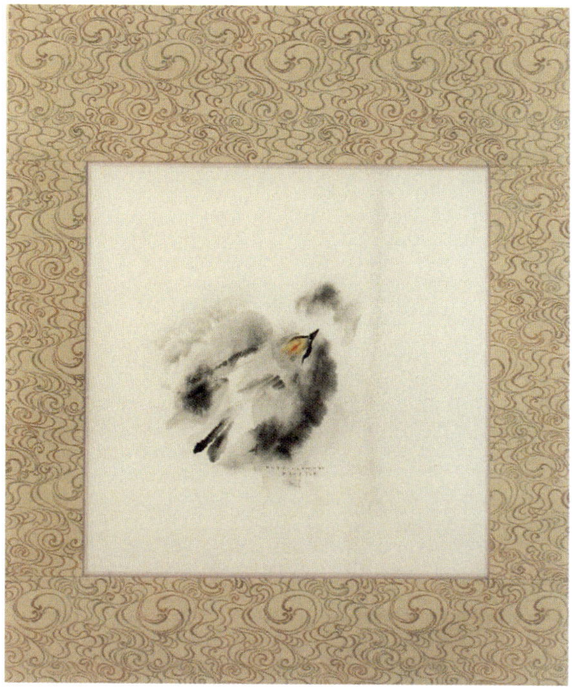

Ruby Crowned Kinglet, 2017, ink and color on paper, silk scroll.
Copyright © 2017 Makoto Fujimura.

small trees that Clayton, my second son, helped plant his first year at P.S. 234, a tree that was scorched by the fireball that had incinerated cars when the towers fell on 9/11.[9] The leaves were gone. The bird was easy to spot. It was a small, olive-colored bird, with a bright red patch on its forehead. I later identified it as a ruby-crowned kinglet. I had never seen a kinglet in Tribeca.

Perhaps, I reasoned, the migrating birds cannot navigate now that the two big "trees" that we called the World Trade Center are gone. I noticed that the air currents had changed. The colder winds blowing off the coast came through directly on the north side of where the towers had stood. I felt the negative spaces in the winds.

The kinglet leaped to the ground as I pondered birds' journeys into the light. It began to sand bathe in the dirt, still with a thin layer of 9/11 dust gathered in the corner of the garden. The orange-red markings flashed in between the turning maple leaves: a flash of stigmata, darting in and out of a small Ground Zero garden, leaving indelible marks on my soul.

Chapter 7

A Slice of Expression

Tokyo University of the Arts, founded by Ernest Fenollosa and Okakura Tenshin, where I spent six and a half years mastering the art of Nihonga, is brimming with extraordinary, gifted art students. In my time there, my peers were people like Takashi Murakami and Hiroshi Senju. The luminaries who graduated from this school of arts and music include Ryuichi Sakamoto (who I would befriend later in New York City), Shigeru Ban, and Léonard Tsuguharu Foujita. Countless young artists, young designers, musicians, traditional crafters, and scholars studied there. I felt most of them were far more skilled and gifted than I was.

Looking back, I feel I was very fortunate to have discovered the limitations of my gifts early on. In such a competitive setting, one may be forced to reckon with deficiencies more than potentials, but in my case, I came to focus on what I began to call my "slice of expression."

My "slice" came about even as an undergraduate at Bucknell University where I spent many hours alone at the Art Barn, located off campus. Perhaps that experience at Bucknell led me to my cur-

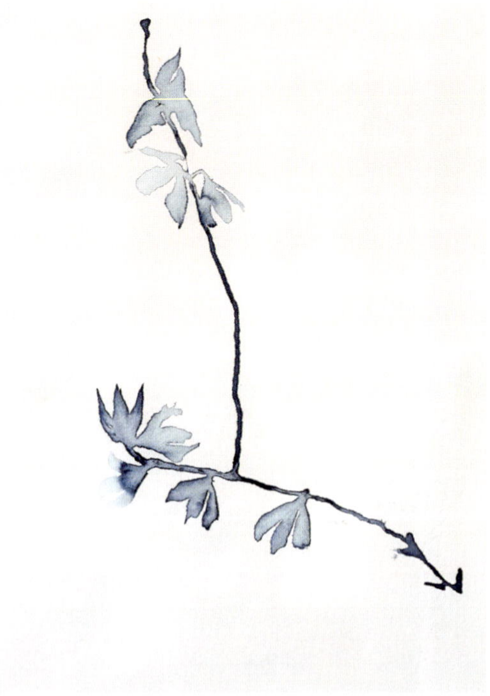

Forsythia, 2020, indigo ink on paper, 12 × 8 in.
Copyright © 2020 Makoto Fujimura.

rent studio, also a converted horse barn. Often, we take our gifts for granted. In class, I would sketch, using one brush to capture a movement of an animal or a figure; I seem to have a knack for capturing, with a single stroke, an essence of an object, figure, or landscape. I call this "essentiation," a word I invented to avoid using euphemistic terms such as "abstraction," which I find a bit confusing.

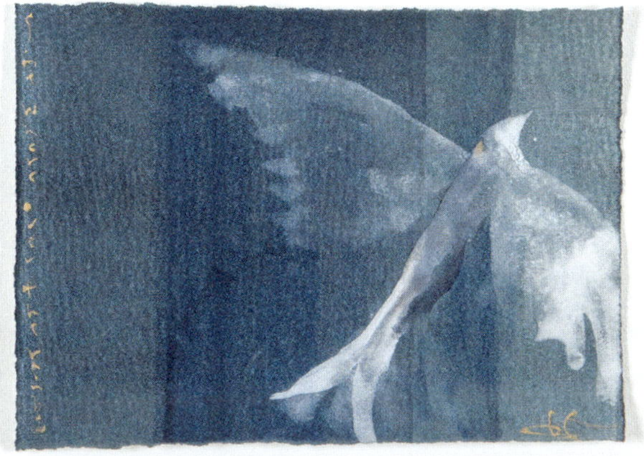

Somewhere over the Rainbow, 2019, mineral pigments, watercolor, and gold on paper, 9 × 12 in. Copyright © 2019 Makoto Fujimura.

I remember painting cows roaming in the fields of Lewisburg, and my painting professor pointing them out in a class as an example of how a brush could be used. When he did that, I was a bit surprised because I thought what I'd done was not anything special: I thought anyone with a brush could do what I did. I remember my peers looking at my "essentiations" of cows and wondering how I managed to capture a movement so well.

By the time I got to Tokyo on a national scholarship to study Nihonga in 1985, I knew that my range of gifts was limited; but I also knew that my "slice of expression" was the only gift unique and special. Fortunately for me, the history of Japanese art is filled with past masters of this type of "essentiation": artists whom I studied, especially Tohaku Hasegawa, Sesshu, and other Zen painters, often painting in spare brushstrokes with sumi (calligraphy) ink; their rich history of "birds and flowers" genre; and masterpieces that I remember seeing in Boston in my earlier days. Even Sen no Rikyū, a more idiosyncratic tea master of the sixteenth century, seemed to capture his world with such "essentiation." Being a National Scholar gave me ample opportunities to study their works up close.

Even though I am now an established artist, I am still, day after day, nurturing my slice of expression. There are still many people more gifted than I am. That has not changed. I was just fortunate to know, early on, my limitations and to work hard to develop my slice.

Every single person has been given that slice. It's important for us to focus through a particular lens on the gifts already given to us, rather than seeking to gain expression over others, or desiring what gifts others have. We need to learn to sing our soliloquies.

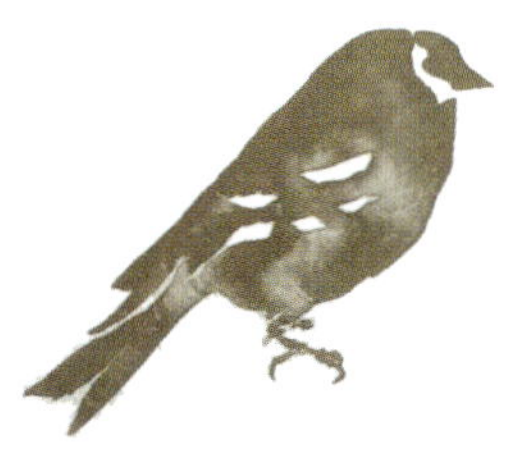

"Goldfinch" outline detail, from
Goldfinch, 2014, limited edition
lithograph print, 12 × 16 in.
Copyright © 2014 Makoto Fujimura.

Chapter 8

Soliloquies

Song sparrows herald the spring with sonorous pronouncements, to celebrate a new season, with a distinct large dot on their rotund chest feathers. When the chest is fully expanded, taking in the fresh morning air for their soliloquy, the dot becomes a blur in the wind. In the late fall, they munch on the browned remains of morning glory seeds and change their tune to close the season with notably somber melodies. Their reflective, refrained notes announce the arrival of a winter.

French master Georges Rouault used the term "soliloquies," noting that he, as a Catholic painter in the "No Exit" (Sartre) modernity of postwar Paris, felt like he was painting and uttering a soliloquy in solitude; but he discovered that, on the contrary, many in history sang the same tune, or felt the same way in an exilic land. He realized that he was joining a chorus of "soliloquies" who attuned themselves to the soul's journey toward the light even in exile from mainstream culture. Instead of the dark, somber portraits of those oppressed by the system, or the bleak streets of Paris seen in front of him, Rouault began to paint modern portraits influenced by stained glass windows of the past.[1]

For an exhibit that featured my works alongside Rouault's paintings in a New York gallery, I visited his estate in Paris.[2] The estate has left the studio intact, as if he could walk in anytime, to continue to squeeze the paint onto laid-out paint knives. I also had the privilege of exhibiting in 2020 as part of the "Georges Rouault and Japan" exhibit at Panasonic Museum in Tokyo as one of the living artists influenced by Rouault. Rouault's lines trace the schisms of postwar Paris, and yet they are pulsating with life and faith. His work is a signpost for those who seek to swim against the current of a time dominated by cynicism and ennui, a signpost toward a colored shimmering light shining into our darkness.

Rouault lived and worked in the outskirts of Paris, then a marginalized area known for the homeless and prostitution. He could have chosen to live in Montmartre, where Picasso and Degas, Matisse, Toulouse-Lautrec, and Renoir hung out. But Rouault chose the path of the solitary. Scholar Thomas Hibbs notes of the origin of this term "soliloquies":

The very notion of a soliloquy dates back to the fourth-century work of Augustine, who coined the term as the title from one of his earliest books, in the year 386, as he made his final transition from paganism to Christianity. As he comments in that work, "Because we are speaking with ourselves alone, I want the book to be called The Soliloquies." In the course of his internal dialogue, Augustine states that the soliloquy is a speech that involves internal dialogue (a searching within the self to uncover the truth

or decide upon a course of action) as well as the potential inclu-
sion of others as listeners and perhaps even as potential dialogue
partners. As the opening quotation from Augustine indicates, a
soliloquy involves an internal searching, a recognition that the self
is a mystery to itself, a mystery whose depths can be plumbed by
"questioning."[3]

Perhaps, as I have found my "Ground Zero" life, living in exilic faith
both in downtown New York City and now in Princeton, I have
found my voice, like the song sparrows, singing my soliloquies.
The natural materials I use resonate with the marginalized, like the
Nikawa history, and pulverization of the outcasts, and generational
gifts of artisans.

Gofun Oyster Shells

Now, at my studio, I am preparing a batch of oyster shell white, called
gofun. Gofun is one of the trickiest of Nihonga techniques, but once
it is mastered, the resulting white is silky and opaque, trapping light
and gossamer transparent at the same time, with a quality of light
no other white can match. Gofun in made from weathered oyster
shells (particularly Itabo oysters) that sit in eastern beaches of Japan
for more than ten years. As I pulverize the pellets made from refined
oyster shells, I can control the opacity by varying the hide glue mixture. Then the powder mixture is made into a ball, and I throw this
ball against a plate more than a hundred times to mix the glue and

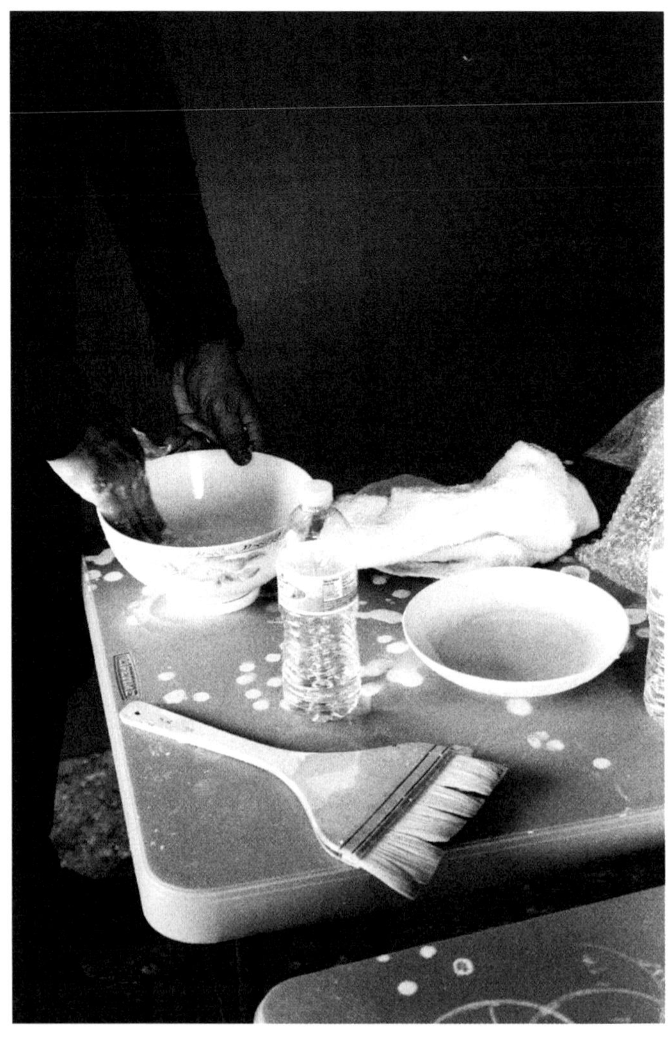

Makoto Fujimura preparing oyster shell gofun in the studio.
Photo credit Alyson LeCroy.

the pulverized powder. The technique is called *hyaku-tataki*, literally "hitting it a hundred times."

The rich history of gofun parallels the history of oysters in other estuaries. Much of the Hudson River, like all the intricate waterways around New York City or Tokyo, is an estuary. In an estuary, saltwater mixes with freshwater, bringing together multiple ecological habitats to form the world's most diverse and most abundant ecosystem.

An Ecosystem

This abundance arises from an environment that is delicately balanced and highly competitive. An environmental scientist told me that while an invigorated estuary contains many pockets of homogeneity—like beds of eelgrass or oysters—it is fantastically heterogeneous. These diverse pockets coexist in a constant interaction, often in competition with each other. And each pocket is subject to the ebbs and flows of the estuarial system, including variations in salt concentration and sediment from the interaction of river and tidal waters.[4]

Estuaries also offer crucial buffer zones for many species. They form a critical nursery area, for example, for young salmon, striped bass, and other fish who come downstream after hatching. Life in semi-protected estuarial wetlands during a critical period of their development readies these fish for life in the ocean.

Oysters are one of the many species that thrive in estuaries. They filter the water for plankton and bacteria to feed themselves, in the

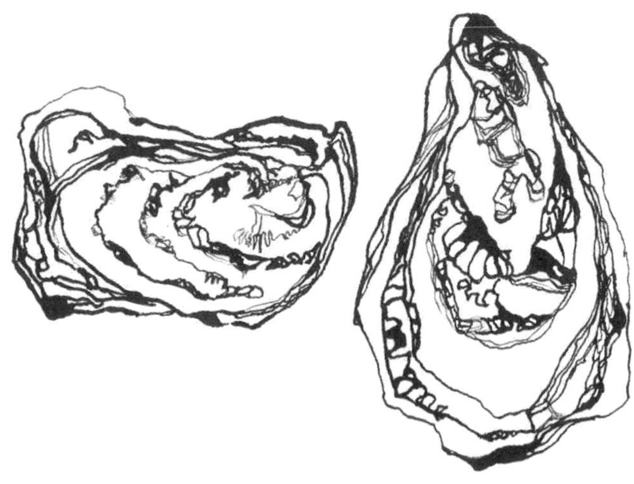

"Oyster Shell" illustration, 2024, sumi ink on paper.
Copyright © 2024 Makoto Fujimura.

process serving a variety of functions critical to the health and diversity of species in the surrounding ecology. These small creatures are remarkably effective at cleaning the water they inhabit. They even turn some pollutants into pearls in the process. But they can purify some types of pollution only at the cost of polluting themselves. Because of their function as natural filters and the fact that adult oysters do not move, they are an indicator species, the "canaries in the coal mine" of their ecosystems.

A feast of gofun mixture, properly made, should echo the cascade and ebb and flow of the ocean waves. This is what Sotatsu's *Waves at Matsushima* painting so masterfully captures.

New York Harbor used to host oyster beds so abundant that New York City in the late 1800s was known for its oysters. The area where I used to jog around the promenades of downtown Manhattan was filled with oyster shacks in those times. But the famed oyster beds were decimated in the early 1900s by pollution and raw sewage spewing into their habitat. When storm surges from Hurricane Sandy in 2012 surprised New Yorkers, the flooding went up as far as 30th Street and destroyed many artworks in the Chelsea Arts District. Had the oyster beds been intact, the natural seawall they formed would have mitigated Sandy's damages. Thus, restoring the oyster beds is now one of the post-storm responses.

I lost more than fifty works in a Chelsea gallery during the storm surge when Sandy struck. Oyster beds would have prevented such erasures of not just my works, but thousands of artworks kept in the basements of Chelsea galleries.

AS I CREATE a "long snake" from carefully stretching the gofun ball, like kneading bread dough to see how well it has been mixed, and adjusting Nikawa glue along the way, I hear song sparrows again, singing their soliloquies. The making process of my slow art materials makes me aware of my surroundings. The flakes of gofun dry as paste onto my hands, and I can tell by the crispness of their pull onto the skin how opaque the white will be on paper.

Estuaries offer a key model for how an artist can thrive. We can think of the river of culture as an estuary, a complex system with a multiplicity of dynamic influences and tributaries. Within it are many nurturing—but not isolated—habitats. Their purpose is not so much protection as preparation. Each individual habitat strengthens its participants to interact with the wider environment, making for a diversity that is healthy enough for true competition.

Artists are like oysters. They breathe in the estuarial mixture of complex influences and cleanse the cultural water; they create aggregated beds of communities of makers to buffer against storms of culture wars; and they create beautiful pearls out of the gritty sand, a "thorn in the side" that sneaks into the oyster's delicate folds.[5] These "pearls" of artistic produce are perhaps seen as gratuitous beauty for the necessity of survival. But we must value them, precisely because they are extravagant and remind us of a world of abundance.

Connected habitats allow for exposure to stronger currents, which push participants to build stronger swimming muscles or grow deeper roots, depending on the context, strengthening each for the overall flourishing of the greater cultural ecology. Each one of us could be one of the small planktons that float in and out of the eelgrass. Yet, each of us plays an essential role for the entire ecosystem to thrive. Our cultural estuary, too, depends on creatures dominant and small, all connected intricately in interdependence.

Through the oysters filtering the water around them—with the by-product of turning irritants into iridescence—a diverse ecosystem can be generative. But beauty is far more than a marginal by-product. And the goal of culture is far more than its sustainability, as sustainability is the minimum baseline of stewardship. As it is in the estuary, culture is generative by nature, and if it is healthy, it should give birth to many future creatures. Artists and creative catalysts gathered like an oyster bed may also contribute to a larger buffer that can serve as a seawall or breakwater against the currents of utilitarianism and commodification, and the torrents of culture wars, that erode our humanity. I call this buffering effect "culture care." Culture care is to see culture as an ecosystem to steward, rather than a battleground to fight over. Culture care is to seek abundance in faith, rather than see the scarcity around us as the only path. Culture care is to create cultural estuaries.

There are historical examples of such cultural estuaries. Sixteenth-century Japan, which produced many art forms, including Sen no Rikyū, as I've noted, became a fantastic cultural estuary as Portuguese and Italian missionaries came into a land of feudal struggles. Early twentieth-century New York City, with exiles arriving from threats abroad, and struggles in the US South, created a mixture of influences that birthed Abstract Expressionism and the Harlem Renaissance. In pre-Renaissance Europe, Ottoman invasions brought a mixture of Islamic and Asian cultures into contact with the West as the Black Plague decimated the population. As I've written previously, even in such bleak times, or perhaps because of such darkness, we see artists like Fra Angelico lead the way to the Renaissance, and eventually lead to Shakespeare and company to build their theater.[6] Salons of Paris in the eighteenth and nineteenth centuries lead the way to Picasso and Matisse, as well as countless artists and writers gathering to create the future of Modernism.

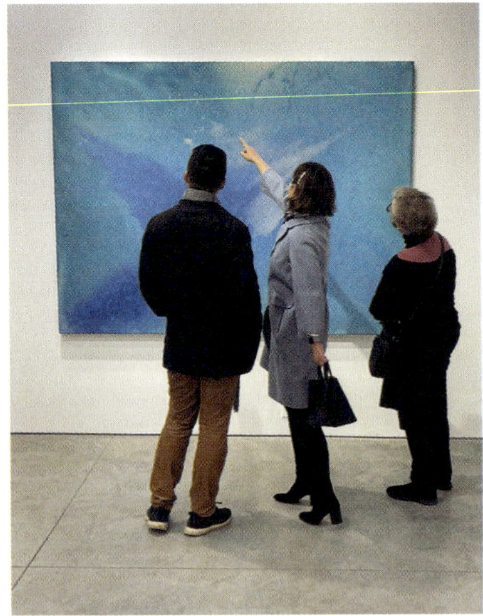

"Re-Sonance" exhibit opening, December 2021. *Christmas 3020*, 2020, white ruby, azurite, malachite, quartz, and gesso on canvas, 66 × 89 in. on display. Copyright © 2020 Makoto Fujimura. Photo credit Makoto Fujimura, 2021.

Defiant Humanism

As I've walked the path of these stone steps into my studio, I now see that I have been given a path to create portals, to dedicate my life to my art, so that future generations can create their own paths and sing their own soliloquies. I've had dark and stormy days when I was not sure whether I could still take that path. In defiance against my own darkness and despair, my body took the path even if my mind could not see the possibility; the discipline of painting embedded in my somatic knowledge carried me on, when my heart and faith failed me. This is the beginning of what David Brooks called "defiant humanism"—creating when the world is falling apart, when one has lost hope, facing the ashes of Ground Zero.

Perhaps our "art"—gifts created so extravagantly and gratuitously in attempting the impossible—is bound to be outsized and impractical for the marketplace or restaurants, so that we will not see such art as convenient. Perhaps art is inconvenient, eccentric in existence.[7] Perhaps cultures are birthed out of eccentric disruptions of extravagance that flows out of our wounds. Mysteries can unveil themselves in front of us, and our eyes open to see our mundane liturgy as a portal to the new. Perhaps my own art belongs not in the transactional market frenzy of the art world, but in a portal that points to our true home, like a teahouse, a Listening Room.

In New York City a commercial gallery in Chelsea hosted a wedding and a funeral on the same week during one of my exhibits. An observant friend said, "You know, I can't think of any other artists in Chelsea in contemporary art where that can happen. Can you imagine getting married, or having a memorial service, in front of Damien Hirst or Jeff Koons?"

That statement made me think. What has happened to our culture, and our arts, where art has deviated from serving a role in key sacred ceremonies that define our lives? Why would contemporary art point only to ironical distance or derision of the sacred? What needs to happen for art to once again provide the backdrop to the theater of everyday lives?

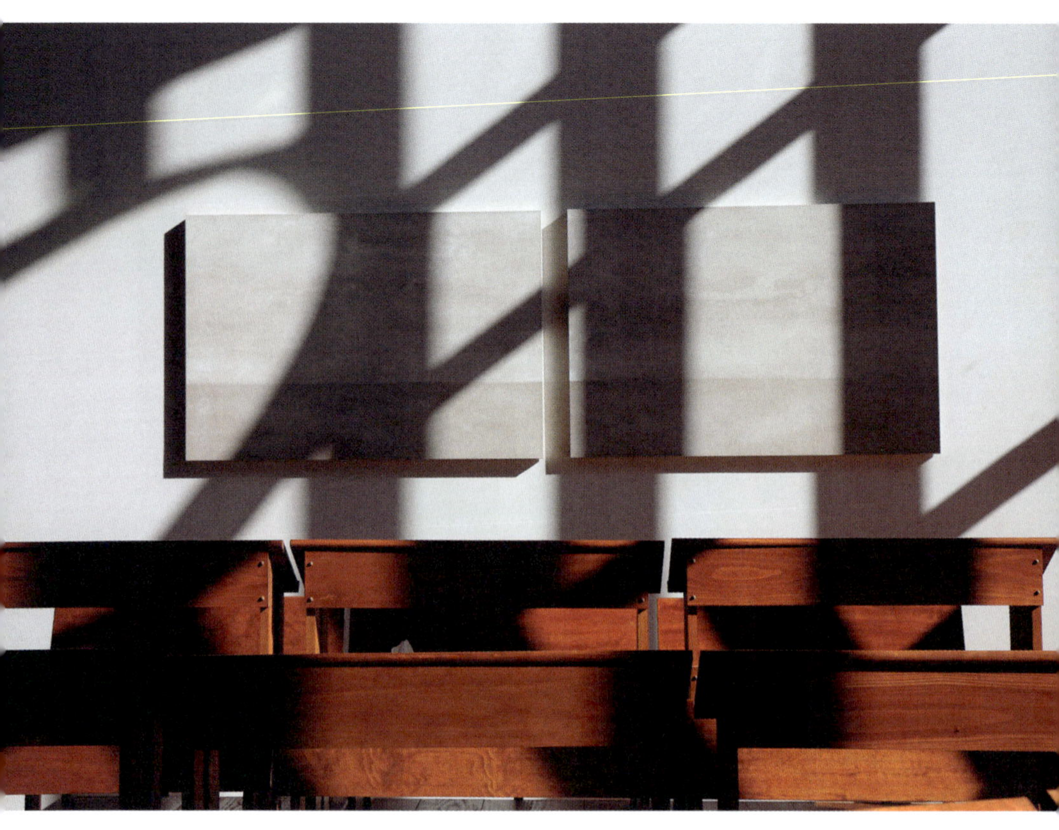

Easter II, 2016–2017, All Saints' liturgical panels installation, oyster shell white on Belgium linen. Copyright © 2017 Makoto Fujimura. Photo credit Alyson LeCroy.

Mark Rothko, in his ideal vision for his painting, stated: "It would be good if little places could be set up all over the country, like a little chapel where the traveler, or wanderer could come for an hour to meditate on a single painting hung in a small room, and by itself."[8] Rothko was right to reject the opulence of the world, insisting on creating a space where a work can be a portal rather than merely a luxury item. Rothko's aesthetic looks to the East, creating a modern synthesis of art that empties itself of self-expression, especially at the end of his journey. The art market is designed to create a spectacle out of "shock," and celebrity artists are featured one season and discarded the next. Rothko's work, instead, is a fragile portal, leading us into a space of generative making, where the gaps can be filled by beauty, fractures can be mended, and gold and colors can be poured. This hospitable space of silence is what I seek in my studio. Such a space is not just so that we can slow down to witness the art of Rothko (or Agnes Martin, or Bill Viola, or Richard Tuttle); it is a space for the fullness of humanity to come to rest and find a vista into new futures.

Painting with Ashes

My own journey of faith and trauma after 9/11 took me to a parish in Princeton, New Jersey, at All Saints' Church. I have donated liturgical works there, sixteen panels to be changed for every liturgical season. When I painted the panels, I was grateful to think of these key moments of our lives being celebrated in front of these panels.

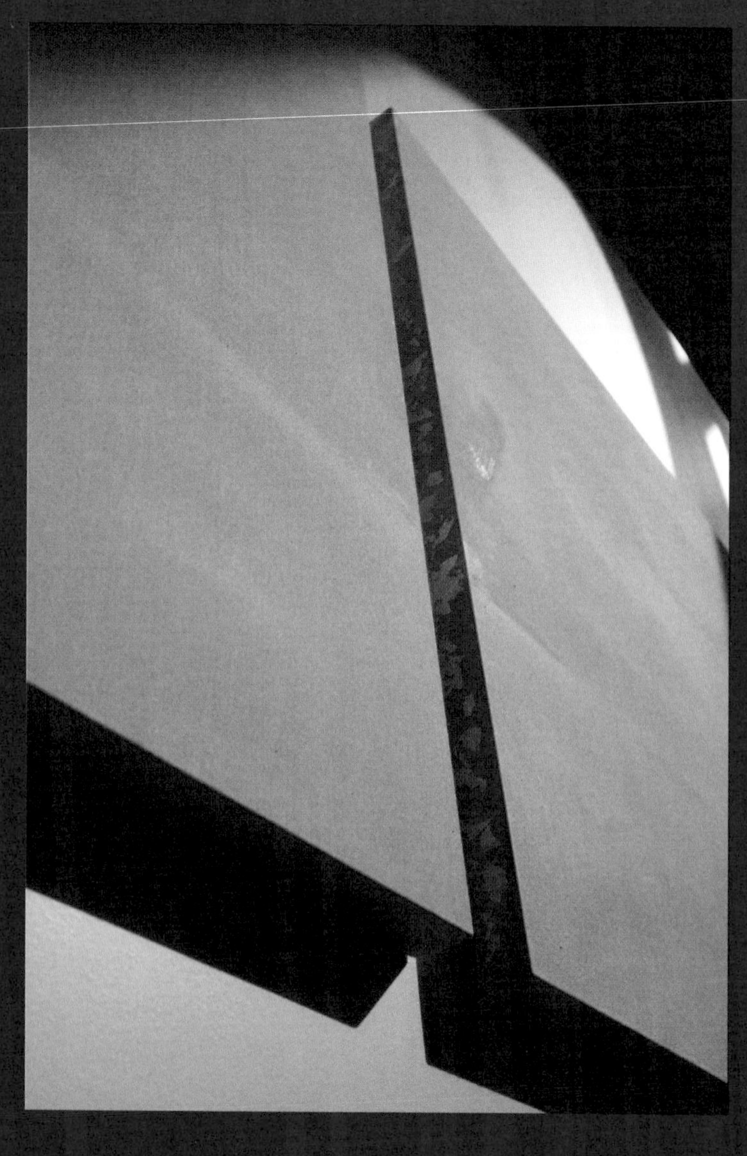

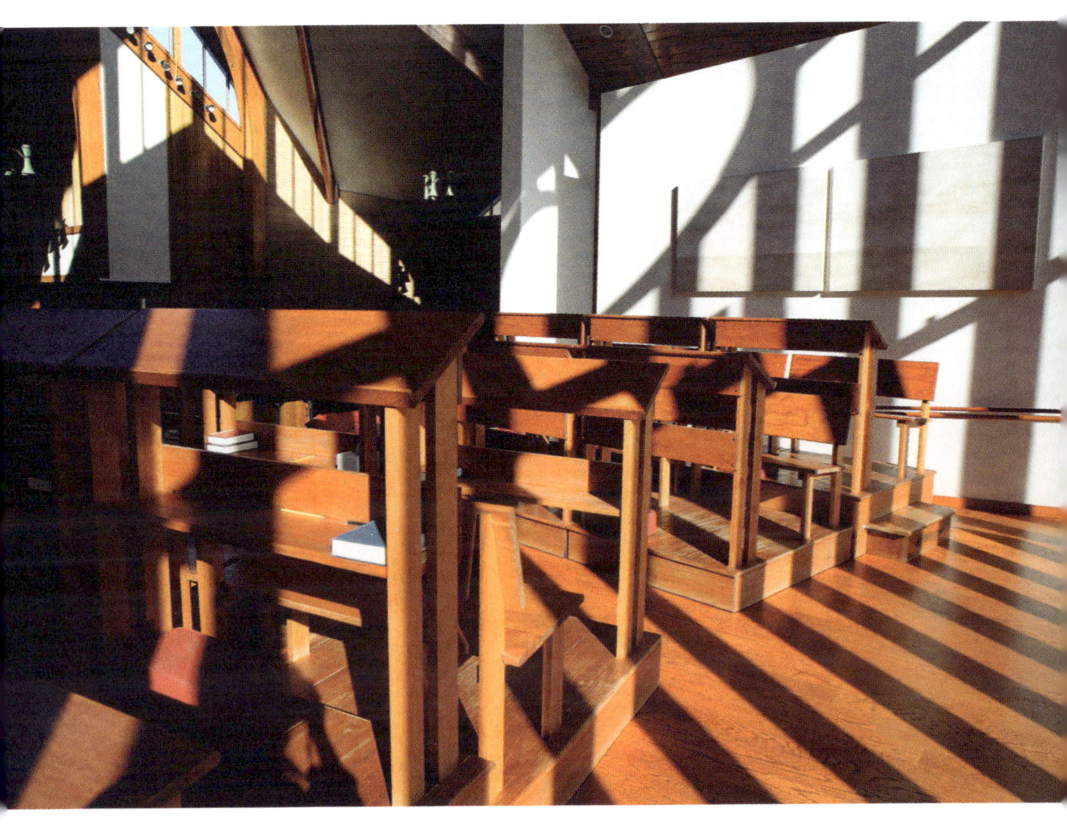

Easter II, 2016–2017, All Saints' liturgical panels installation, oyster shell white on Belgium linen. Copyright © 2017 Makoto Fujimura. Photo credit Alyson LeCroy.

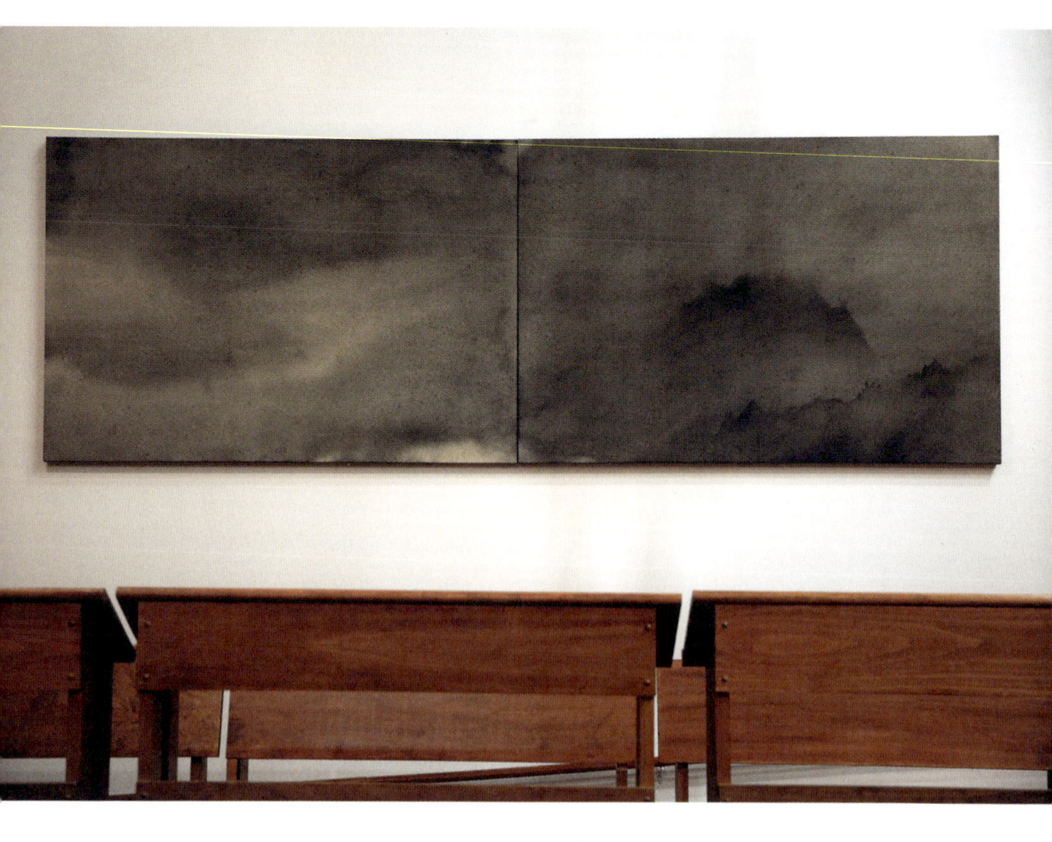

Lent—Ash Wednesday, 2016–2017, All Saints' liturgical panels installation, mineral pigments on Belgium linen. Copyright © 2017 Makoto Fujimura.

In God's grace, I would myself be part of the community's journey to grieve losses and celebrate marriages. My mother's memorial service took place there, and her remains rest in the church cemetery. I remarried in front of those panels. They also silently witnessed the pandemic shutdown.[9] To create these panels, I had to work with faithful church vestry members and congregants to find a way that ordinary people not trained in museum or gallery practices could handle the works and think of their lightfast qualities and durability.

The morning and afternoon slanting light comes over the paintings, and the shadows of the window with the cross move across them. Since they were designed for worship, I did not want them to be works that compete with other elements of worship, such as the choir or communion table at the heart of the church. Later, I realized that since I had to develop a durable but quiet expression through the materials I use, these All Saints' paintings became the bases of many of my more recent works. What you do in service often allows generative growth in expression. We are defined by what we create in love.

When I worked on the Ash Wednesday panels for the beginning of the penitential Lenten season leading up to Easter, I began to do layers of dark washes of a hundred-year-old sumi ink used traditionally for calligraphy. As I was working on these panels, pondering the Lenten season of self-examination, I realized that sumi ink is compacted pine soot with Nikawa. I was literally painting Ash Wednesday panels with ashes. "Ashes to ashes, dust to dust," I hear as I receive ashes on my forehead. Art is also making New out of our beautiful ashes and dust of pulverization.

Chapter 9

Interdependence of Colors

What is light? What is color?

I learned in my color theory class in college that these questions are much deeper, and more complex, than I had assumed.

Light, we know from modern physics, is both a particle and a wave. We can model light as an electromagnetic wave or as a stream of photons. What is strange is that these are contradictory models that cannot coexist. One mathematical model called Maxwell's equations describes a relationship between the electric and magnetic fields. Another using Planck's constant describes the photon model.

What I inferred, as an artist, is that these complex theories, which the brightest of scientists wrestle with, show that these paradoxes, an "impossibility" in "provable" scientific and mathematical models, can coexist in mystery. With even a rudimentary knowledge of quantum mechanics, we can behold simultaneously contradictory theories together in a single phenomenon of light. I wonder, again as an artist, whether these paradoxes are not "problems to be solved"

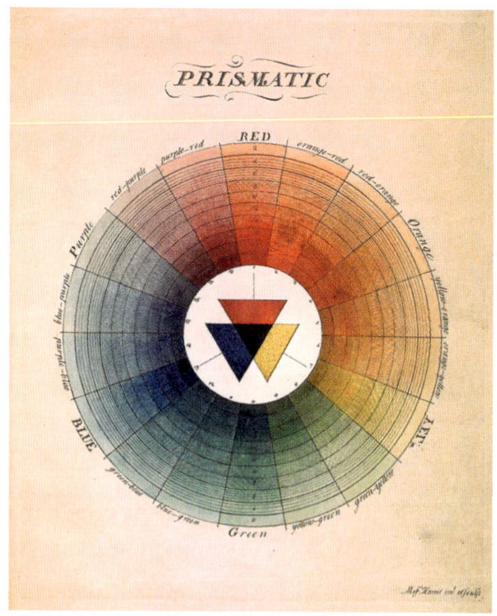

"Prismatic Color Wheel" engraving,
Moses Harris, from *The Natural System of Colours*, 1776, plate 1.

but ways to train our imagination to hold in tension the paradoxes of
reality. It is an exercise to hold complexity in our minds, accepting
the mystery in creation.

Why is this important? Art delves into a mystery of creation and
of a deeper knowing journey.[1] Art develops the imagination to move
away from false binaries and accept multiple models simultaneously
operating within a single work. Our senses, and the confluence of
our somatic inputs, seem to point to our capacity to have multi-
dimensional and multilayered thinking. In our days, narratives to

defend established positions often lead to the demonization of "the other," in our typical "we-versus-them" mentality. We may establish certainty in such contested positions as valid, but what if, just as the light itself shows us, there is more than one way to explain a single position? Who will paint the whole picture, rather than each part seemingly contradictory to, and warring against, each other?

In my color theory class, we used the book *Interaction of Color* by Josef Albers. Albers, known for his iconic *Homage to the Square* series, taught at Yale University from 1950 to 1958 and (with his wife Annie, who was also a brilliant artist) influenced countless artists who studied there. In this book, and in this class, we learned further about color complements. Colors such as yellow and purple, red and green are complements on a color wheel (according to the color theory of Johannes Itten, who was Albers's teacher at the Bauhaus school in Weimar). Albers connected these color relationships to uniquely capture relational realities. He considered his *Homage to the Square* a combination of squares in various relationships to each other, a series of abstractions to be a type of portrait done through pure color. Cezanne and Matisse used color complements well in their paintings, contrasting the reds and greens of fruits or hats, to create vibration in the painting of lively joy.[2] But at the same time, as I've noted, there is impending decay and the looming natural cycles of death and life. There is psychological tension in any artist's use of color, and such tension is what Albers described well in his teachings.

If color can begin to capture our personhood, even in the monochrome of a square color combination, then the relationship depicted

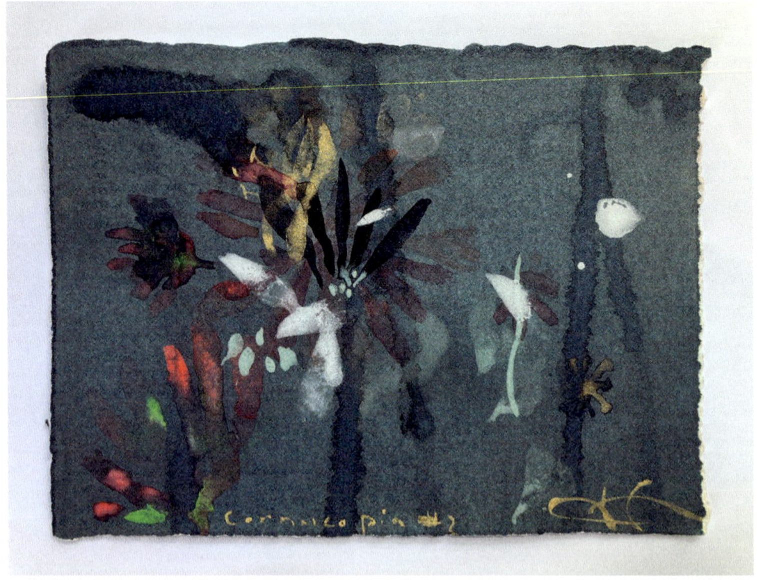

Mercy's Garden—Cornucopia #2, c. 2019, mineral pigments, watercolor,
and gold on paper, 5.5 × 8 in. Copyright © 2019 Makoto Fujimura.

between colors can represent a particular community as well. True personhood can be described either as a healthy dependence upon others, as in a tight-knit family, or as independence from others, as we mature in our gifting. Albers's *Homage to the Square* captures the interaction of both the dependence of colors and the independence of each square. Colors are *interdependent*.

A community needs to provide both a sense of belonging and nurture unique identities, and cities, as a collection of communities, are even a more complex matrix of dependence and independence. What fascinates me is that colors operate strictly in an interdependent paradigm and refuse to be reduced to binaries (black and white) or remain isolated. Why is that important? Again, color theory applied to art and life can be a culture care antidote to our tendency to create false binaries and prejudge and scapegoat each other. Colors teach us that we cannot stand alone and isolated if we want to show our true selves.[3] Color theory also relates to the abundance of an estuary ecology, which helps us to map out how we may move away from culture wars to culture care.

Colors exist both dependently on and independently from other colors. We, too, should navigate this complexity—not fragmented in isolation but communally interdependent while being distinct individually. Art is the journey through this kaleidoscopic mystery of coexisting, prismatic colors spreading into the world. I call this the "principle of interdependence" journey toward the light.

Hummingbirds often dart in and out between my rose bushes and gladiolas, a cornucopia of summer flowers. I am told that hummingbirds see colors that we cannot see, and that they are attracted by ultraviolet light and refractive colors in gardens. Perhaps I am drawn to colors that I cannot see, and yet feel their presence with my inner eye. They are (as Emily Dickinson might note) "humming-birds," playful emanations in the world of migrant navigation, "a route of evanescence."[4] Colors that we cannot see (yet) may guide us toward that new path of complexity and joy.

Mineral pigments, detail. Copyright © Makoto Fujimura.
Photo credit Stephen Proctor.

Abundance

Art is the gratuitous abundance of Creation flowing into our limited domains. We may react to "transgressive artists" as making us
uncomfortable, or we may celebrate and deride them because they
are shocking and start a culture war boycott. Artists are sometimes
conscripted in the front lines of culture wars and intentionally

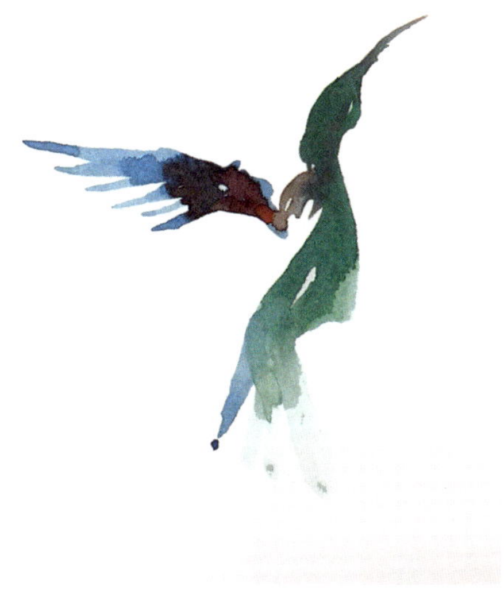

Humming-Bird, 2019, mineral pigments, watercolor, and gold
on paper, 6 × 6 in. Copyright © 2019 Makoto Fujimura.

create transgressive art (but sometimes they volunteer to fight on those front lines as well). Such works, driven by "fifteen minutes of fame," do not last. But enduring art that creates into the divide can often give us new paradigms, principles of how we see that we can learn from, helping us to sanctify our imaginations to create a more robust, and abundant, future.[5]

Nihonga materials, furthermore, expand the color wheel. The refraction and coarseness of minerals create even more complex permutations of colors. Just as we can train our brains to reject false binaries, to be generative, to "think in colors," we can develop our vision for prismatic refractions that move beyond even the conventional color schemes.[6] A hundred layers of minerals—like layers of sacrificial prayers offered toward abundance despite the obvious scarcity facing us, especially in the dark slums of the world—can paint the lives we have lived, in our common journey toward the light.

A Journey into the Dark

Japan is at the end of the Silk Road; India is at the beginning. A kimono worn in Kyoto is the natural design descendent of the sari worn in India. I noticed that many of the Nihonga masters pointed this connection out in their paintings. Artists such as Ikuo Hirayama and Sawato Fukui, both were professors at Tokyo University of the Arts, championed it and traveled to India frequently and created the "Silk Road Movement" in Nihonga salons. When I had the opportunity to accompany my wife, Haejin, to serve in India with her organization Embers International, which helps generations of human trafficking victims, I experienced a reawakening to my own journey in Nihonga and to a reality of encroaching darkness that surrounds us.

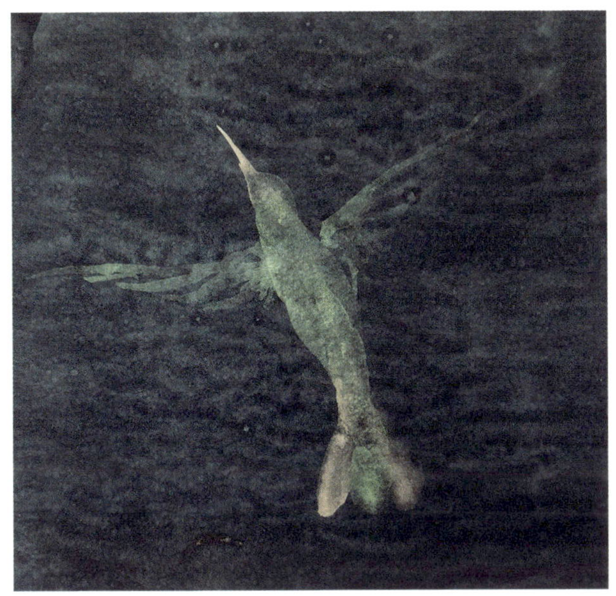

Mercy's Garden—Humming-Bird #3, 2019,
mineral pigments, watercolor, and gold on paper, 6 × 6 in.
Copyright © 2019 Makoto Fujimura.

Chapter 10

Jacob's Ladder

Art is finding the light in the darkest of realms. Before we departed for India, I stood before a painting that confounded me. For several months, I had layered the painting—eighty-nine by sixty-six inches—with pulverized malachite and azurite. I then used a technique to create golden wave patterns to undulate on the surface. But in doing so, my intuition pushed me to take a risk of creating a golden "veil" that split the image in half. This overlay, even though the surface was exquisite, created a visual conundrum, one that I did not know how to resolve. I pushed the painting as far as it could go, thereby pushing myself into a borderland of impossibilities. Often, an artist stands at the edge of an abyss, and experiences both despair and the thrill of such a threshold.

Even as we landed in Mumbai, with moist, tangy air filling the atrium of the airport, and as we lugged our luggage onto a bus, the mystery of the painting stayed imprinted in my mind's eye.

Mumbai is a feast for the senses. The blaring horns of rickshaws and small trucks filled the streets, with the orange flags of political fervor waving past our bus windows left and right. As we walked under the relentless sun, spices and stench mingled with the aroma from the *dosa* batter crisping in vendors' carts. We were led by my wife's team to one of the largest brothel areas, where a faithful group of people who serve the women living and trapped in the brothels guided us. In that strange light, cacophony and pungent air colliding, my soul began to awaken like a winter bulb beneath the hardened soil.

As we climbed up the creaking staircase, it became darker and darker. I felt the narrow corridors press in as if the light were being sucked out with oxygen. The farther we climbed, the darker it became. We turned the corner in the balcony of the third floor, and intense sunlight blinded us.

A woman in a blue sari, the color of the highly pulverized azurite I use, limped out of one of the "stalls." She spoke in a whisper, recounting how the ministry guiding us had helped her to recover from a severe burn and holding up her disfigured left hand. Suddenly, a woman rushed into the next room with a client, a young man dressed in designer shorts as if he were on a beach vacation. We were made constantly aware of other activities around us by the menacing creaks of the bustling steps and floors beneath us. The woman seemed oblivious to it all and continued to share in her whisper. The stall, not more than five feet square, became a buffer for us to listen. I noticed that there was a ladder behind her, a ladder that would take her and a customer into a darker loft space of violation. The ladder seemed handmade and a bit narrowed at the bottom, making it look upside down.

We were invited to pray with her, and it was my turn to pray. As I

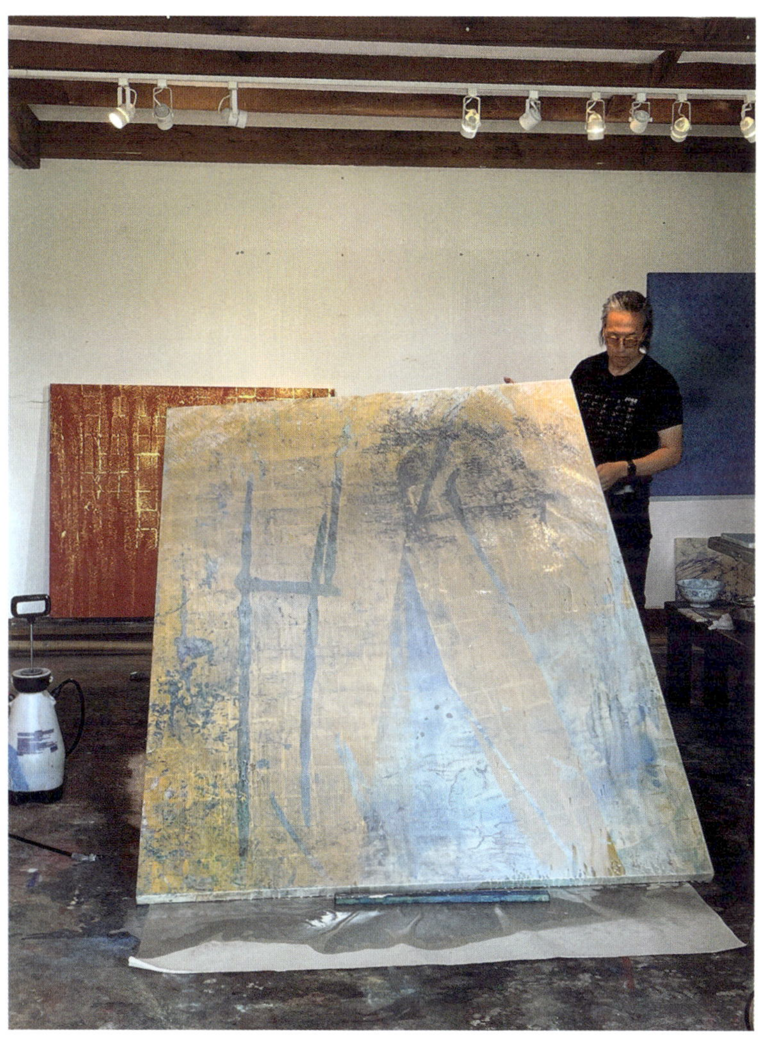

In-process photo of *Jacob's Ladder*, 2022, gold, mica, quartz, and white ruby on Kumohada paper over canvas, 89 × 66 in. Copyright © 2022 Makoto Fujimura.

began to utter my feeble prayer, the ladder kept on intruding in my mind, and as if to push this intrusion away, I opened my eyes slightly. Then, I thought I saw a golden light descending upon this upside-down ladder. I closed my eyes to pray, and opened them again; the light was gone. I realized only after that there was no window, but pure darkness, up in the loft.

What did I see, even for just a moment?

The ladder, in my mind's eye in prayer, turned into a Jacob's ladder, with angels ascending and descending on it (Gen 28:12). My uttered prayer hoped that this golden light would release our sister and saturate this room. My art often begins in prayers facing devastations, the "ground zero" of our lives. Even a feeble prayer can open the eyes of my heart. I realized that I had seen that ladder before. It was at the heart of the "conundrum" painting I was working on back home. God gave me a vision in Nihonga materials.

In the dark brothel in India, I saw visions of white ruby, quartz, and mica. I have used white pigments, including white ruby and quartz, as symbols of sacred purity, of the veil that is lifted when the Spirit illumines our hearts. I realize now, as I reflect on this experience, that the slow process of preparing gofun sanctifies my imagination, as if the pulverized Itabo oyster shells can cleanse my vision.

I had to travel nearly eight thousand miles to see *through* my eyes, to understand my own painting. The materials and visual movement I struggled against, perhaps, was so that I could pray that prayer in prismatic white splendor, to see an incomplete Jacob's ladder completed in prayer.

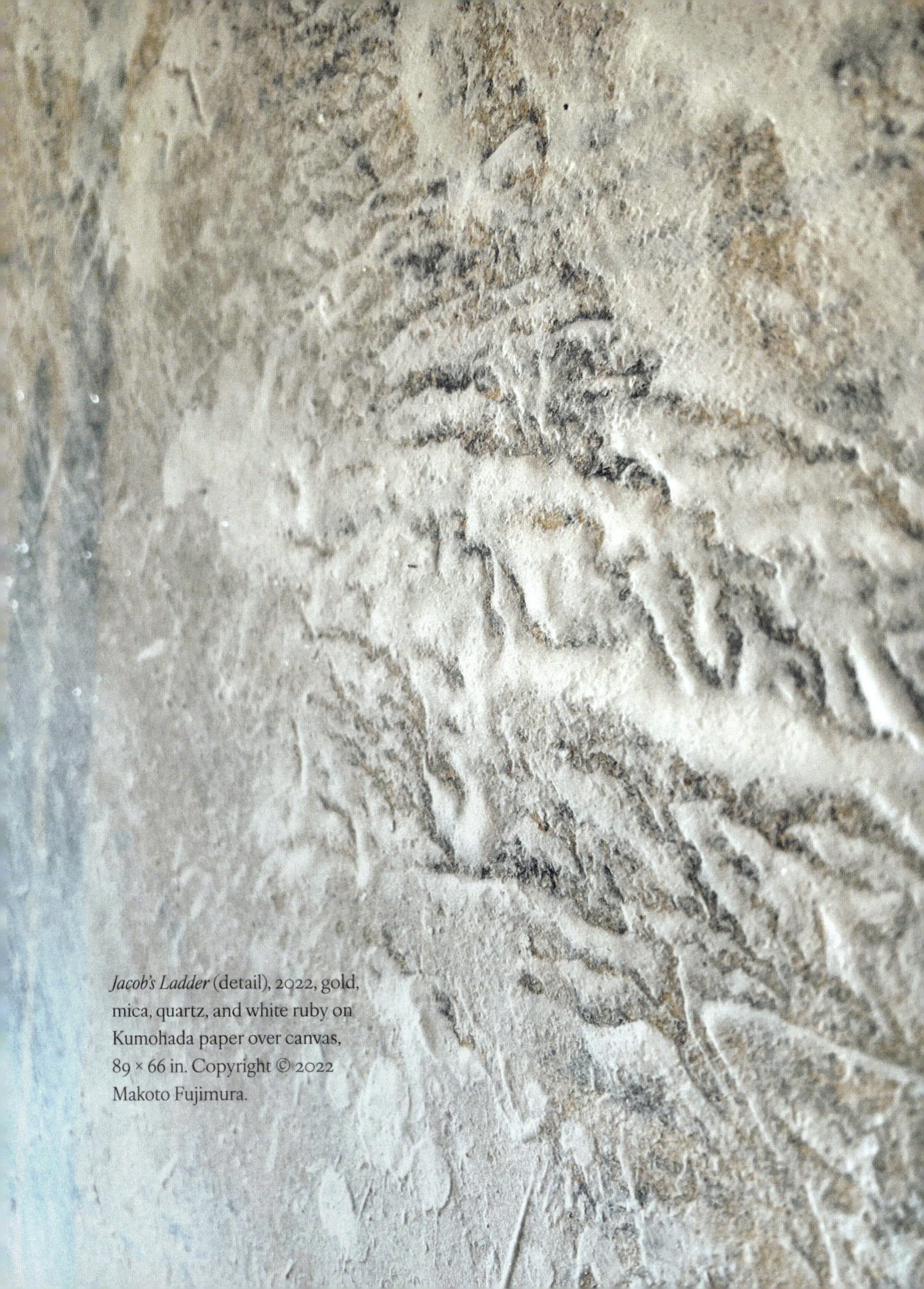

Jacob's Ladder (detail), 2022, gold, mica, quartz, and white ruby on Kumohada paper over canvas, 89 × 66 in. Copyright © 2022 Makoto Fujimura.

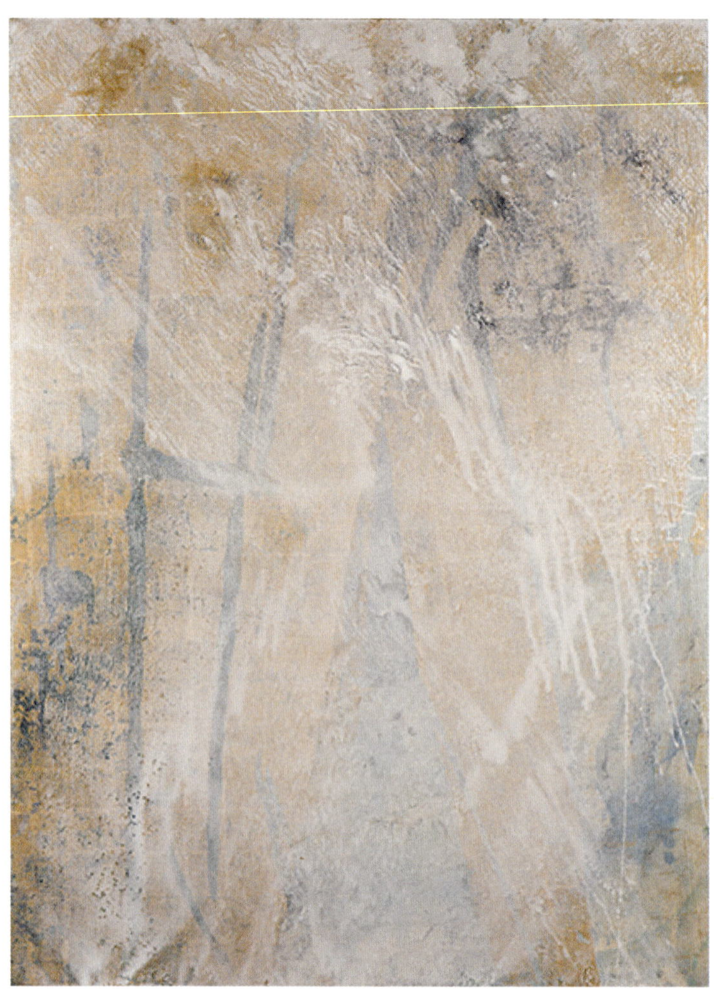

Jacob's Ladder, 2022, gold, mica, quartz, and white ruby on Kumohada paper over canvas, 89 × 66 in. Copyright © 2022 Makoto Fujimura.

Miraculous Discoveries

Art documents our miraculous discoveries. As soon as I got home, I prepared the materials I "saw" in that vision in the brothel and painted. I invited the same film crew that had accompanied us to India, and they continued to document the process.[1] I poured the oyster shell, white ruby, and quartz pigments on top of the surface that already had more than a hundred layers. I painted what I had seen in the brothel while praying, and that prayer became the painting—*Jacob's Ladder*.

As I experience these miraculous discoveries, I am more and more convinced that in art, time warps in strange ways. Time can "slip" and art can become a portal of eternity. Perhaps linear time can be bent backwards like the spoon of a magician or Dali's clocks. I paint what I intuit, and often future events complete the work in a way that I could not have possibly imagined. Materials often lead the way. This has happened before, as in the painting *August 30th 19:33*, painted in the darkness of my soul, and many paintings I have done in the past.

My life with Haejin is now drawn into the traumas of precious lives halfway around the world. God, the only true Artist, lovingly crushed me over the years, so I can now be fully God's "material," to be invited to participate in the Spirit's prismatic prayer to the darkest corners. Art can be a portal toward the impossible, a magnificent longing manifested into the world. Art is a mystery revealed.

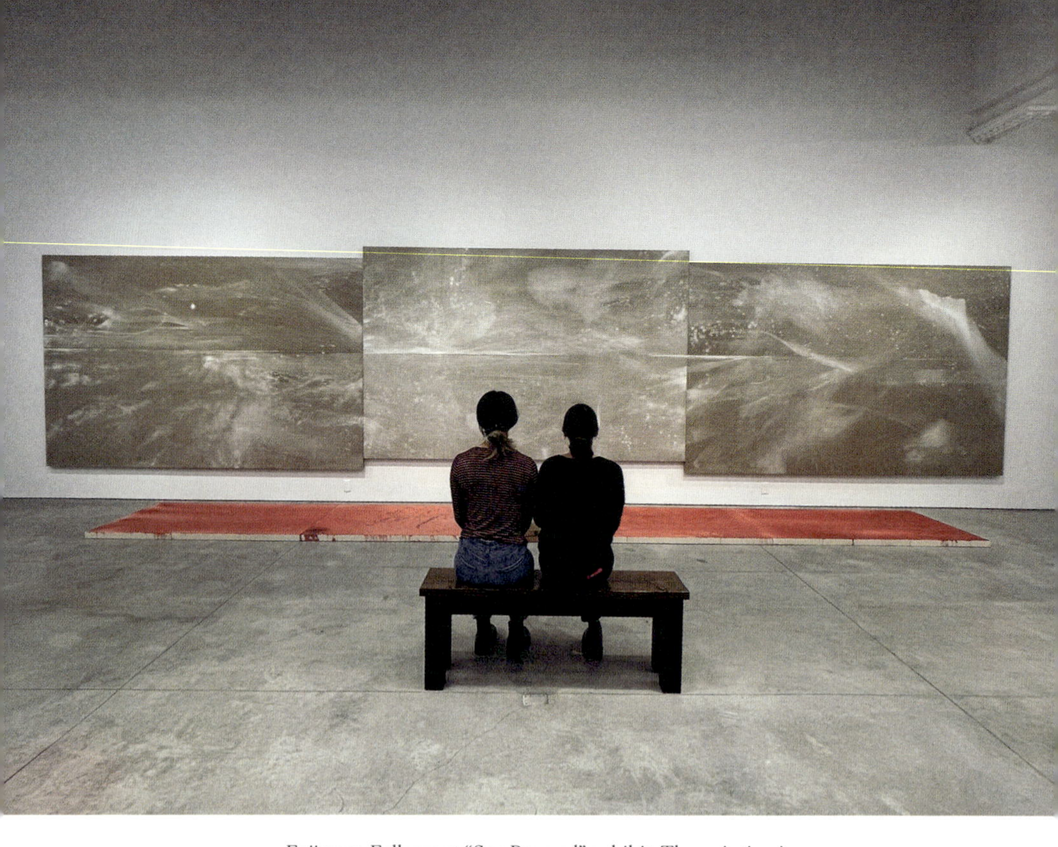

Fujimura Fellows at "Sea Beyond" exhibit. The painting is
Sea Beyond (triptych), 2019, oyster shell on Belgium linen,
84 × 396 in. Copyright © 2019 Makoto Fujimura.
Photo credit Makoto Fujimura.

Chapter 11

A Magnificent Longing

A Spontaneous Gospel

Can we transcend the barriers erected between cultures and traumatic histories through art? How can an artist's visions help us to see beyond the most difficult challenges of our days? I experienced such sonorous possibility at Yokohama Museum several years ago, a visit during which I took one of my Fujimura Fellows, September Penn, and her husband, Ivan Penn, to Japan.[1]

September is a pastor/singer-songwriter, and Ivan is a journalist. Together, they have been producing a theater production, *Sounds of the Civil Rights Movement: The Power of Song,* taking the songs of the American civil rights movement to public awareness, lifting music in the fissures of our racial struggles. I have been journeying with them with my slow art approach and have walked with them into their struggles and efforts during the recent spike of racial violence. Part of my work is to collaborate with music that came out of trauma and discrimination, out of the brokenness of their "Kintsugi" journey.

I often mentor outside of classrooms, in my studios and in my travels. My fellows and interns follow me to my business meetings in galleries and museums. They work with me in the studio. We mend broken vessels and learn Kintsugi together. In one such journey, I had a business meeting at Yokohama Museum in Japan where my art was to be exhibited. I shared with them about the piece, an installation called *The Resurrection 2,* which takes up an entire wall at the museum; it's a series of long rectangular panels inspired by fumi-e (the "stepping blocks" mentioned in Chapter 3). I spoke on the aesthetic connection between fumi-e and Kintsugi.

I asked September to be in her "prayer mode," to listen. Though she would not have understood Japanese, I sensed that she would be able to pick up the essence of our conversation through her highly attuned intuition. I have found that people who have suffered well have highly attuned senses of what is happening spiritually in a room, even if they do not speak the language. In the museum, I told the staff about Japan's Christian history, and of the biblical narrative, what I call the "theology of making," and of fumi-e and Kintsugi.

I turned to September as the meeting was ending and spontaneously asked her to sing. I often surprise my mentees by challenging them this way. I want them to trust their intuition, and boldly create into the moment.

"I do have a song to sing," September said, as if she had been anticipating my challenge. She got ready to sing, and one of the curators stopped her, asking, "Can we bring our other colleagues to hear this?" We nodded, and within a few minutes, what seemed like the entire staff of Yokohama Museum filled our small office.

Then, September's sonorous, powerful voice resonated into the hallways and echoed beyond into the exhibit rooms. She pierced the silence of a museum with a "Kintsugi" song, which we later called "Through His Brokenness":

It's through His brokenness I've been made whole.
It's through His brokenness new life unfolds.
He takes the pain from my past secrets untold,
And fills me up with gold, through His blood, I'm pure gold.

He saw me falling.
He heard my cry.
Gathered me up
Right by His side.
He takes the pain from my past secrets untold,
And fills me up with gold, through His blood, I'm pure gold.[2]

I asked her, "Where did you find that song? That was indeed perfect!"

"I just composed it in my head ... it just came to me!" she said.

Incredulous, I asked her, "You mean just now?"

"Yes," she beamed with her wide, wonder-filled eyes, "it just came to me!"

As I explained to the museum staff what had just happened, many stood in tears. This, as I've explained in my book *Art and Faith: A Theology of Making,* is a New Creation story, an unraveling of the mystery of the gospel into our world.

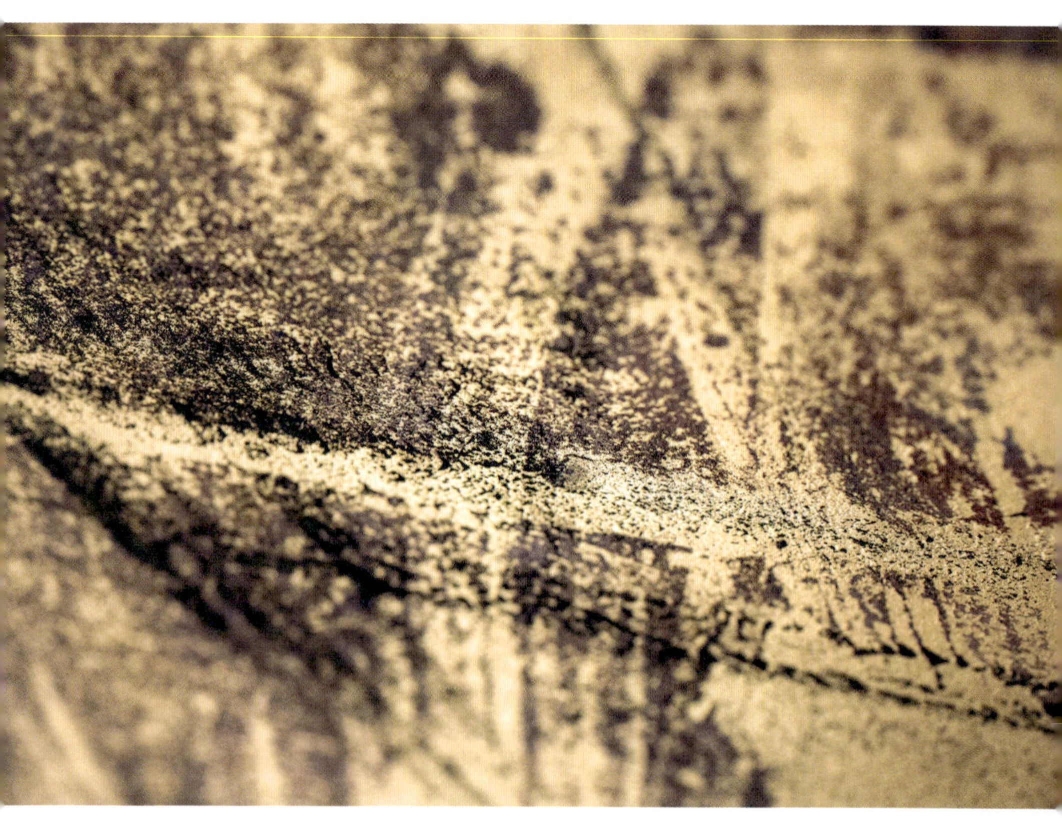

Gold macro detail. Copyright © Makoto Fujimura.
Photo credit Windrider Productions.

Song

The plight of African Americans and their generations of pain have birthed gospel music, or what Pete Seeger called "the power of song." This powerful music arose out of the fractures of African American generational struggle. Their music had to be a spontaneous offering, without much instrumentation. Their "training" was the daily rhythm of resilience and resistance within. The very communal and yet personal pains created a cultural condition that turned their traumas into the music for the masses. Their voices invited not just their own to sing, but others who long for liberation to sing with them. That may be why, in Japan, one of the most popular choirs to join is a gospel choir. Literally hundreds of these choirs exist, with many housewives joining them. September and Ivan brought into the high museum culture of Japan a spontaneous composition, bringing the power of song extemporaneously to a foreign culture.

Japanese history possesses wounds from generational traumas, both because of being horrific aggressors themselves and as the only nation that has experienced atomic destruction. An American gospel tradition harmonized with the Japanese history of the fractured being mended, overlapping with Kintsugi tradition. My art reveals the fractures of a Japanese American, inheriting the history of unjust internment in our own land, thus recognizing the racist histories of nations with which I am associated. Yokohama Museum's collection of my works anticipated, perhaps, a moment when September's faithful making broke open the silence of mutual traumas.

The end of Dr. Martin Luther King Jr.'s famed "I Have a Dream" soliloquy came about when he put aside the civil rights legal arguments that he had begun the speech with on that fateful moment at the Lincoln Memorial. As I note in *Culture Care,* Dr. King's friend, the singer Mahalia Jackson, stood behind him and implored, "Tell 'em about the dream, Martin! Tell 'em about the dream!"[3] Dr. King rose to the occasion, put down the text, and began to preach from the heart. The extemporaneous vista he painted with words and oratory skill is what we recollect now. Without this "art of the extemporaneous," we may never have remembered that moment or the march to the extent that we do today. We now see the "I Have a Dream" speech as the central vision of the beauty that flows into our call for justice today.

In the oppression of slavery, African American culture had to develop resilience. The extemporaneous ability came about due to generational, compounding traumas. The power of African American songs has proved to be one of the greatest gifts of our time. Such songs are dandelion seeds scattered in the wind of racism, effusively offered in unfathomable suffering. Now such seeds have traveled far, to take root even in foreign lands.

In our journey toward the light, we too must reorient our lives to be able to "preach from the heart." My art has been a path to discover that myself, by dying to self, to create portals for others so that they may discover their paths as well. My art is a journey toward a dream greater than my own, into fractures and brokenness both visible and invisible. September's song flowed out of that dream of Dr. King's many years ago. All art paints the vista of a greater dream, painted for our communities and future generations. Culture care is to create communities of estuary harbors where these vigorous dreams can be preserved, nurtured, and given wings.

Our art needs to be a "dream portal" for all viewers who behold our art. That portal may be the drawn lines of hope and tears, leading us to a life well lived, a journey into the light, to exhort others to create a movement of care. That journey is to remind people of what hope we are marching toward, to reach into the deepest recesses of our own visions toward that ember of light. Artists who operate as border-stalkers can exhort the world in this way, in and out of preserved tribal languages into a visionary, collaborative, extemporaneous "jazz" language of the heart.

After September sang at Yokohama Museum, I called several people in our network of musicians in Tokyo. We booked a recording studio to capture her song in a demo. A young jazz pianist accompanied her. The impossible dreams begin with the music of collaboration across nations. This has led to further collaboration in Los Angeles, to a live painting with Yukari and Keiko Yanaka performing Rikyū's tea ceremony.[4]

The path to peacemaking, the path to the studio, begins in our intuitive, collaborative making. Such an effort to activate our imagination has power to change and define the future. Every time we make, we are framing the future. We can create more weapons of mass destruction, or we can create beauty that endures. The unfulfilled dreams of the countless victims can manifest themselves in what we make, whether that be art, music, theater, dance, cuisine, or peace. Their souls cry out even now through us.

After so many years of living and working in what is Ground Zero,

I began to ponder whether even such a place of deep and lasting trauma can be seen from a different perspective. Can Ground Zero be a true zero cancellation point, a Genesis ground out of the cruel calculus of past evil and losses? Can Ground Zero be a place of redemptive seeds of lost lives that can take root now? Rather than our devastation point becoming a detonation point to incite more violence, can we see that there is an opportunity to reverse the inevitable cycle of violence upon violence?

Koi

Silent Spring, Rachel Carson's seminal book on environmental stewardship, opens with a town with no birdsongs—an image of the bleak reality we are facing if we continue to poison the earth. After many years of culture wars, we also have a "silent spring" of those who are not ideologically driven to sing anthems of culture wars but are rather the "salt of the earth" minority, standing in the margins singing their soliloquies.[5] These people, many of them marked by creativity, will be hard to measure by polls or statistics, because by their very nature, they are hard to categorize and refuse to be forced into the binary metrics of algorithms. The poison of culture wars has decimated the lyrical soliloquies of artists. Just like DDT and other pesticides continue to haunt the environment, culture will continue to suffer from the toxins now ubiquitous in the air.[6] The idea of culture care comes out of artists singing their soliloquies into the poisoned air. I had to have faith that culture's rejuvenating power, and the generative human ability to create something beautiful out of our traumas, a Kintsugi culture, can still carry us to a rejuvenated cultural soil where our scattered dreams can take root. For me, as a Japanese American, such a journey, drawing into the Ground Zero ashes, takes me into a deeper introspection.

In a small gallery in the Ground Zero area created by a local art historian a year after 9/11, I installed a video piece rear-projected onto Kumohada paper (the same paper I used for *Water Flames*) called *Nagasaki Koi*. This video was taken soon after that fateful day of 2001 when I was invited to travel with friends to Nagasaki, a true Ground Zero. As we meandered into the museum built upon that Ground Zero, I noticed a small pond, with gigantic koi swimming about. I slowed down the video and reversed it, so the koi are swimming backwards, their enormous tails gyrating the water with wakes disappearing into the surface. In projecting it, I raise a question: "Can art reverse time?" What kind of culture can we create for future generations to steward song sparrows, oysters, and Kumohada paper?

Nagasaki Koi is a visual prayer: a prayer of resistance to the regression of entropy and decay, the erosion of hope, and the voices of cynicism that veil our impossible dreams. Prayers can utter impossible dreams, even if our culture cannot. It is a prayer to see Ground Zero as a genesis point, even a countdown to zero to eliminate nuclear weapons, to pause our violent acts, to even consider the reversal of atrocities and destruction. As I've found in my own Ground Zero journey, living and working there can be a starting point for our journey toward peace. Art can "reverse" time, not in the sense of going back in *chronos* time, but in a sense of seeing *through* the eye, not merely *with* the eye. When we do that, we will peer into *kairos* time, the Timeful reality where dreams are manifested into the ashes of Ground Zero.[7]

My art is a prayer labyrinth of memories, allowing viewers to trace the complexity and mysteries of what I see, drawing future paths of caring for culture, to paint the vistas of the dreams I carry. The words of this book are dandelion seeds, designed to disappear into the winds of our culture. Perhaps by being labyrinthine and category-less, and deeply process-driven, my work and my life may not be understood for some time, if at all, in the marketplace of art.[8] Somewhere, somehow, these scattered seeds will take root.

Just as Rikyū devised a liturgy of peace during a time of feudal war, my art and my journey are a slice of expression of God's grand vista, to the spreading Ground Zero realities all about us. This book grew out of an artist's observation, how an artist sees. Such an intuitive and complex matrix of vision pushes back against the false binary judgments we make of each other, and the reductivism of the algorithmic transactions of our data-mining social media. Art grows our dreams to create a new world. May our art be a true sacrificial offering at the altar of dreams—dreams of plenty. Just like the splendors of *Nagasaki Koi,* the slow gyrations of resplendence, a Ground Zero pause. Art, as the reverse current of dreams from our brokenness, is a golden river whose "streams make glad the city of God" (Ps 46:4).

A Path Home in the Light

I step out of the studio and the bluestars greet me in the greying light. The feathery branches, waving in the gentle October wind, are now bright, pungent yellow. Goldenrods illumine the paths to my right, and several rods have snuck up in between the boards of my studio steps, now incandescent in the dusk light as I walk back to my farmhouse.

This book became my journey into the light, beginning with a wandering paragraph in which I tried to capture my experience still awaking from the slumbers of the global coronavirus pandemic. Much has been lost, and I see my own grief captured in the goldenrods of autumnal hues, in the waning light of October. A book like this is formed in the darkened womb of the "remembrance of things past," or perhaps in a re-membrance reconnecting the fragmented pieces afloat in the murky oceans of things that have passed. Some things have disassociated, sunken into the depth of the tidal sediments. Surprisingly, in the routine of everyday paths, innocence protrudes, like the goldenrods between the step boards, inviting my attention and gaze. I see fractal light breaking between the tiny flowers, a speck of delight, and I am then, improbably, overwhelmed with joy. I see myself as a child again, wielding the brush saturated with a splendor of colors, enthused at the spreading watermarks, but somehow, quite miraculously, managing the flow to allow permanent edges to form. Art is my return, in meandering strokes of certain love and gaze.

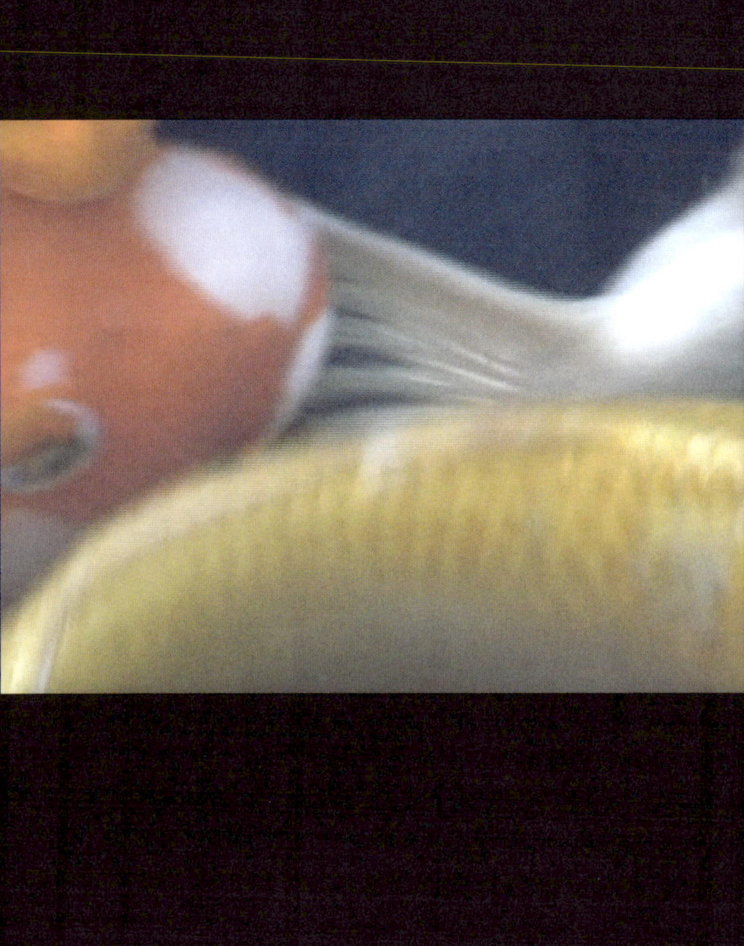

Still from *Nagasaki Koi* video, originally
taken in 2003 by the pond next to the
Nagasaki atomic bomb ground zero site.

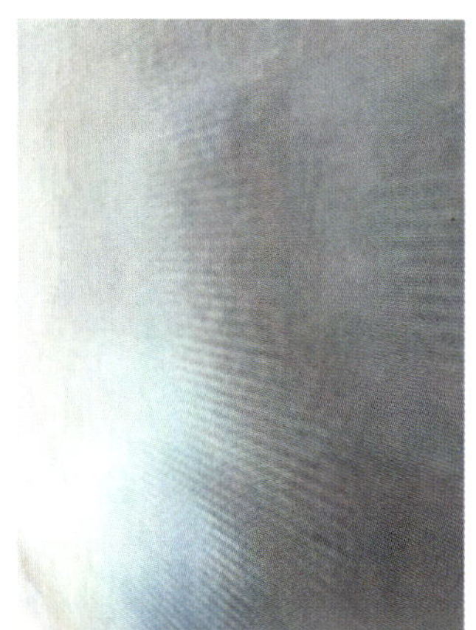

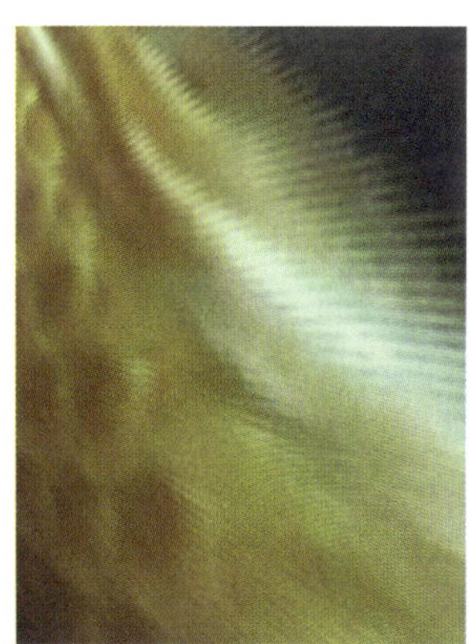

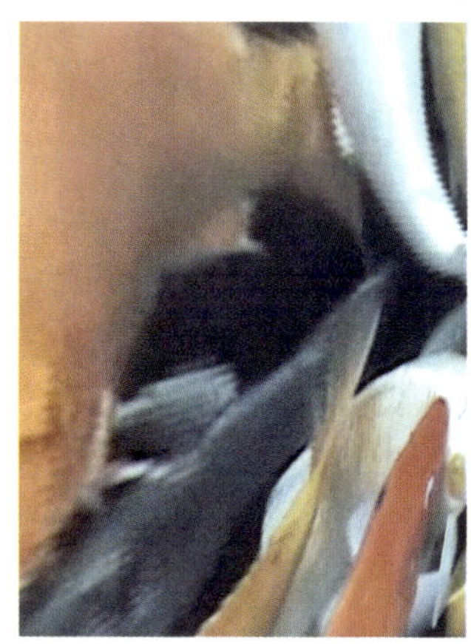

Stills from *Nagasaki Koi.*
Copyright © 2003 Makoto Fujimura.

Definitions

"Culture care," "theology of making," and "common curse" are all expressions I have coined toward a generative discussion. These terms are implicit throughout this writing, and yet I may not explicitly define them so it may be helpful to do so here.

Culture care is to see culture as an ecosystem to steward, a garden to tend to, rather than a battleground to fight over. (See my book *Culture Care: Reconnecting with Beauty for Our Common Life*, 2014.)

Theology of making is to see God as the first and only True Artist and the Bible as a "making" book toward a New Creation, to frame the biblical gospel as a story of Creation–Fall–Redemption–New Creation. (See my book *Art and Faith: A Theology of Making*, 2021.)

Common curse is part of Reformed theology's "common grace," which blessed all human beings. As part of God's grace, we share in the blessings (Matt 5:45 KJV: "That ye may be the children of your Father which is in heaven: for he maketh his sun to arise on the evil and the good, and sendeth rain on the just and on the unjust"), but at the same time, we share in the curses, such as the COVID pandemic we have gone through and the continuing endemic we suffer. Everyone reading this book was directly affected by COVID-19. Through common suffering, we can develop empathy with even strangers across the globe.[1]

In addition, "Behind the Veil," which follows, articulates the origins and manifestations of the approach of seeing *through* that I have developed as an artist. In writing, often these "appendix" sections are the central hidden thesis of a book. In Shusaku Endo's *Silence,* for instance, what is translated as "appendix" is not delineated as such in the original text; that is, there is no separation between the text and the historical narrative at the end. When William Johnson translated *Silence,* he added the word "appendix," so not many realize that the historical notes are the beginning point for Endo.[2]

Behind the Veil

Section 1: My "Inversion" into Jesus

Through the process of painting and encountering enduring art, I "inverted" into faith in the mid-1980s. A flow of grace coming through me that I did not own or fully control began to open the "eyes of my heart." But it would require an encounter with a British artist/engraver to fully embrace my journey into the light.

When I reread William Blake's last epic poem *Jerusalem* on a cold February day in 1986 in my small apartment in Futako-tamagawa (Twin Rivers of Tamagawa) in the outskirts of Tokyo, I heard in Jesus's voice, streaming through Blake's poetry, the same eternal echoes I felt in my studio, the "flow" that I sensed in my heart. Blake writes:

Albion said. O Lord what can I do: my Selfhood cruel
Marches against thee, deceitful, from Sinai & from Edom Into the
Wilderness of Judah to meet thee in his pride.
I behold the Visions of my deadly Sleep of Six Thousand Years,
Dazling around thy skirts like a Serpent of precious stones & gold:
I know it is my Self: O my Divine Creator & Redeemer.

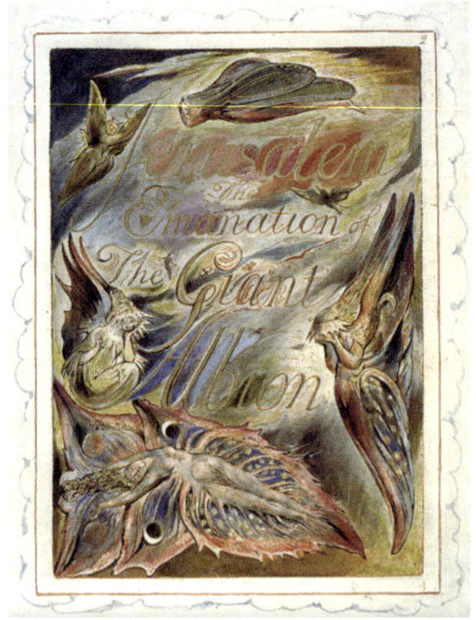

William Blake, *Jerusalem: The Emanation of the Giant Albion*, Copy E, Plate 2, relief etching with watercolor additions. Yale Center for British Art, New Haven.

Jesus replied. Fear not Albion: unless I die thou canst not live:
But if I die I shall arise again & thou with me.
This is Friendship & Brotherhood: without it Man Is Not.

So Jesus spoke: the Covering Cherub coming on in darkness
Overshadow'd them & Jesus said. Thus do Men in Eternity,
One for another to put off, by forgiveness, every sin.

Albion reply'd. Cannot Man exist without Mysterious

Offering of Self for Another: is this Friendship & Brotherhood?

I see thee in the likeness & similitude of Los my Friend.

Jesus said, Wouldest thou love one who never died

For thee, or ever die for one who had not died for thee.

And if God dieth not for Man & giveth not himself

Eternally for Man, Man could not exist, for Man is Love,

As God is Love: every kindness to another is a little Death

In the Divine Image, nor can Man exist but by Brotherhood.[1]

In awakening from a slumber of six thousand years, Albion confesses that "my Selfhood cruel / Marches against thee, deceitful." I identify with this confessional cry, especially with the line "like a Serpent of precious stones & gold," the exact materials of Nihonga I've come to love. In my case, the more I tried to self-express through my art, and using the precious minerals ("precious stones & gold") of Nihonga, I truly felt unworthy of them. The more I tried to define my own self-identity through them, the more I felt this "flow" ebbing. I realized, for the first time, when I read these verses, that I was, somehow, marching against my Maker, even unknowingly, if I made art into an idol of my own making by focusing on "self-expression" and worshipping art.

If Albion's words became my own, then Jesus's answer directly spoke to my heart: "Fear not . . . unless I die thou canst not live." And the following lines after that opened my heart: "Jesus said, Wouldest thou love one who never died / For thee, or ever die for one who had not died for thee." My "conversion" was a "transfer of allegiance" from Art of Self to the Art of Love exemplified in Jesus's definition of love: "And if God dieth not for Man & giveth not himself / Eternally for Man, Man could not exist, for Man is Love, / As God is Love."

My "conversion" was also an "inversion"; I assented to what I already knew in my senses to be true—that in making art, I sensed this flow of the Spirit, but I could not, up to that point, intellectually assent to Jesus fully. But through the pursuit of beauty, I inverted into faith—to know that love is at the heart of all things, and I had been moved by Jesus's words, "Greater love has no one than this, that a person will lay down his life for his friends" (John 15:13 NASB). Love is connected with this sacrifice. In Japanese aesthetics, especially after Sen no Rikyū, beauty has always been connected to sacrifice. It made sense to me that if God is indeed Love, then God's incarnate Son will lay down his life for his friends.

Section 2: Art Is to Create into the New

My art is a portal into a New Creation. What do I mean by "New Creation"? Theologian N. T. Wright states that "we are living examples of the New Creation" breaking into the old. All true artists are trying to depict a new paradigm, a new category.

What do I mean by the word "new"? There are two words in Greek for "new"—*neos* and *kainos*. They both point to the generative, with *neos* pointing to the future, and *kainos* pointing to the renewal of the past; but in our postindustrial lens of a transactional economy, we have begun to lose the potency of these words. We tend to think of the new only as the transactional new of a production cycle, evidenced, for instance, by the word "neon" (a derivative of *neos*). A *kainos* path is an enduring path, one that requires quiet focus to tap into. Our "attention economy" fully utilizes the "neon" to attract attention: a flashy but temporary distraction that offers so much more than it can deliver in terms of our long-term satisfaction.

In *Art and Faith,* I quoted 2 Corinthians 5:17 (ESV), when Saint Paul states: "Therefore, if anyone is in Christ, he is a new creation. The old has passed away; behold the new has come." Apparently, the more accurate translation here is "if anyone is in Christ, NEW CREATION!"

Kainos is the Greek word used here in Pauline epistles for "new creation," but when we hear the word "new," we immediately think of something being improved, as in a new iPhone or a new car. Such is the modern interpretation of the new, or "neon"—that new fashion, new technology, new flashy something that will illumine in culture for only a short time. Both *kainos* and *neos* point to "New Newness." Many attribute this Newness to be a transformation, like a caterpillar becoming a butterfly. Yes, it is transformation, but it's more that: it's *transfiguration* (the Greek *metamorphoo* of Romans 12 is used in the Bible for what is commonly translated as "transformation"). I may even go further and say that *kainos,* in the way that Paul uses the term in 2 Corinthians, is not just a new species, but a new concept of what a species is. *Kainos* is the resurrection, what happened on Easter morning. Jesus's body was not resuscitated but resurrected—that is Saint Paul's emphatic position. Saint Paul is reminding followers of Christ how we are already a "new [*kainos*] creation" as the resurrected Christ enters our lives. When I speak of generativity, I am speaking of the potential, as a result of this historical reality, that affected *all of humanity*, that each one of us, even in our ordinary days, whether we are religious or not, is a portal for this *kainos* creation, the New Newness. Art is, fundamentally, an "impossibility," the impossibility of Easter morning. That impossibility manifests through the Spirit in three New Creation paradigms: (1) the wounded body of Christ resurrected as the New Creation Realm, (2) the "upside down" reality of God's "strength . . . made perfect in weakness" (2 Cor 12:9 KJV) as a "Kintsugi" creation, and (3) our ability to create into the light emanating through the Wounds of Glory. I also believe that such potential is often whispered in the margins of human experience by atheists and agnostics alike, in the gratuitous, in the discarded, in the exiled voices of poets and artists . . . and the homeless, and those trapped in the scourge of generational human trafficking. The *kainos* beauty can break out among the poor and the oppressed (Jesus himself created a kind of exceptionalism for the poor and oppressed, as exemplified in the Sermon on the Mount [Matthew 5]), among those who mourn and those who are poor in spirit, like a Kintsugi vessel. All artists seek the New; great ones redefine what Newness is.

To make the journey even more challenging, our digital neon modes of communication delimit visual data into previously established marketable chunks. If one takes a photo on a digital phone, it is already part of a predetermined algorithm created to form marketable categories and exclude information that is considered irrelevant. Therefore, I paint images that are impossible to reduce or be re-created on a digital screen, surfaces that cannot be captured in digital bits. Art is to provide an antidote to reductive machine processes. As technology becomes more generative and multifaceted, it would be up to our arts to provide a way to create New Newness with that advanced technology and push back against speed and biases that dehumanize.

The assumption that such machines can "beat" and replace humans has caused fear of our tech future. I have argued in the past that no matter how well such machines can perform their efficient tasks, they cannot aid in growing or satisfying our souls, or, as this book attests, learning to see *through* the eye. Because the efficiency of the machine-made world is ultimately interpreted through our lens of neon "newness" of utilitarian pragmatism and efficiency, and measured strictly in the values created by transactional realms or propaganda values, enduring art and experiences are not likely to be captured by the current reductive applications of the algorithmic patterns. We may, in the days to come, drive around in autonomous cars, hands-free, and we will then need to ask ourselves, "What are we creating? Where do we want to go?" If we chase after self-seeking, flashy pleasures, we will be able to get to that reality quickly, but *neon* pleasures are ultimately numbing, fading away with ever shorter intervals of the pulses of sensations. If we want the enduring beautiful reality of ultimate fulfillment to all our senses, we need to "train our senses," as a hard and long journey toward ultimately more fulfilling ends. Machine algorithms can be used to facilitate our growth, just like exercise machines help us to strengthen, and make flexible, our bodies.

Interestingly, though, recent developments in pattern-matching capacities of word-based algorithms reveal that machines have made these interfaces "generative" to create surprising "creative" and even "spiritual" variances. As an artist, I welcome these mysteries. No matter how much an enormous pattern-matching capacity to gather and organize information is at our disposal, we still must discern what is Real using our senses. This Real with a capital *R* is what William Blake points to in his visionary poems. This cultivation of the greater awareness requires that we develop and grow in our sensory, somatic knowledge, and become comfortable in multiple perspectives. Ironically, what cannot be captured in the reductive, transactional market, what will initially be "use-less," will perhaps be more enduring and valuable in the end. Emily Dickinson's poems or Vincent van Gogh's paintings were considered "use-less" to the publishing market and salons of Paris, but their works are more enduring to us because they both created into the New, giving us a new definition of what a poem or a painting does.

Artists are strange creatures in the domain of predetermined outcomes and digital bits. We see so much more than what we can capture with our digital devices or process adequately by linear, rational means. Process-driven, slow art resists such an algorithmic pretense of being able to capture a greater reality by reducing outcomes. It stubbornly remains analogue and slow, generating ever more complex, but beautiful, paths, and at the same time claims the "impossible" feat that transcends flashes of time. Artists (and liberal arts education) are now ever more critical for creating our educational future, and as an antidote for our tech-filled culture war journey that only creates anxiety and fear.

Section 3: Tabasco Sauce and Color Theory

The design on a bottle of Tabasco sauce has not changed much since its first appearance in 1868. If a design does not change over time, it proves the brilliance of the design.

So why is it iconic?

Taking a color theory class helps us to understand why the designer of the Tabasco sauce bottle intuited the power behind complement color schemes, even though the design came before color theory had been fully articulated (we see color charts as early as the eighteenth century [see the color wheel shown in Chapter 9]). The design does something that a color theory teacher will tell students NOT to do in painting. The teacher will say *not* to mix or put complementary colors next to each other because they vibrate off each other and create a jarring sensation to our eyes.

What are complementary colors? Remember that they sit on opposite sides of the color wheel. They are the reddish orange (actually the color of urushi mixture used in Kamakura-bori craft) and

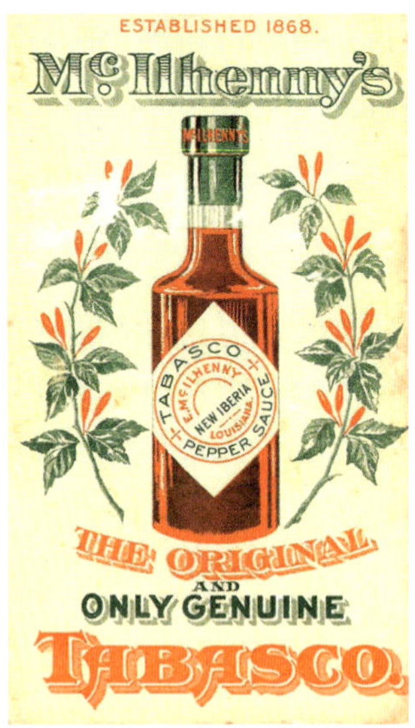

Advertisement for Tabasco sauce, 1905.
McIlhenny Company Archives, Avery Island, Louisiana.

darker green of the Tabasco sauce bottle, and they can cause havoc in the visual field by creating an uneasy dissonance. The designer of the Tabasco sauce bottle intentionally used this dissonance. And it works.

When the Tabasco bottle sits on the shelf, what do the reddish orange and dark green crashing colors convey?

Spiciness.

The brilliance of the design does not end there. The designer took advantage of the reddish orange color of Tabasco sauce to make this unique color combination. In other words, the hot sauce itself in the glass bottle works as part the design.

When I visit policymakers in Washington, DC, to advise them on culture care issues, I carry a little bottle of Tabasco sauce with me for my "elevator pitch" about culture care. If given a minute with a leader, I quickly explain the color theory of complementary colors, and the brilliance of the design, and give them the little bottle. I tell them, "This is what democracy should look like . . . spicy!"

People may assume that culture care, as part of a peacemaking thesis, avoids conflicts. Avoiding conflicts is what Ken Sande, the author of *The Peacemaker,* calls peace-faking.[2] Estuary complexity is fantastically competitive, and its vigorous diversity is created out of multiple pockets of interdependent conflicts. True peacemaking stewards such competitive but invigorated ecosystems to nurture the future of expression into communities.

If I have more time with these policymakers, I also explain that artists like Matisse intentionally used complementary purple and yellow, or red and green, all the time. I may even offer to take them on a tour of the National Gallery so we can see the paintings that masterfully use or break these rules. Despite what art teachers advise students not to do, master artists use such "spiciness" in their art all the time. Creating disruption in the system is part of art—and part of the art of governance, of coexistence. Art can teach us to be good leaders and politicians.

We need master "artists" in leadership roles who know how to steward the "complements." Great leaders like Abraham Lincoln and

Dr. Martin Luther King Jr. had the flair of an artist and used words in the same way that complementary colors are used by master artists. Their voices convey urgency and beauty; they are not afraid to take on complexity, stewarding prismatic shards of ideals given to them, a refractive splendor of enduring vistas that they could not reach.

Notes

Chapter 1. Thresholds

1. William Blake, *Jerusalem,* ed. E. R. D. Maclagan and A. G. B. Russell (London: A. H. Bullen, 1904), plate 55, line 51.

2. See Makoto Fujimura, "The Resonance of Being," in *Refractions: A Journey of Faith, Art, and Culture* (Colorado Springs: NavPress, 2024).

3. See Madeleine L'Engle, *Walking on Water: Reflections on Faith and Art* (Wheaton, IL: Harold Shaw, 1980).

4. I was appointed by President George W. Bush to a National Council on the Arts position, 2003–2009; in 2022 and 2023 I had speaking engagements at the Houses of Parliament and to members of the UK Parliament and other world leaders at the inaugural event of the Alliance for Responsible Citizenship (ARC) in London; see Matthew 2:12.

5. See Makoto Fujimura, "The Aroma of the New" (2011 Belhaven University Commencement Address), June 15, 2021, https://makotofujimura.com/writings/the-aroma-of-the-new-2011-belhaven-university-commencement-address.

6. Gaston Bachelard, *The Poetics of Space* (New York: Penguin, 1964), 33.

7. In biblical terms, this is the Holy Ghost. Tim Keller (recalled from our conversations): "We need to be possessed by the Holy Ghost, so as not to be possessed by evil spirits."

8. A "purpose-driven life" (Rick Warren, *The Purpose Driven Life* [Grand Rapids, MI: Zondervan, 2002]) should account for meandering artists who create purpose-less art intentionally!

9. "He lived serenely, as an artist greater than all other artists, scorning marble and clay and paint, working in the living flesh. In other words, this peerless artist,

scarcely conceivable with the blunt instrument of our modern, nervous and obtuse brains, made neither statues nor paintings nor books." Vincent van Gogh to Emile Bernard, Arles, on or about June 26, 1888, in Leo Jansen, Hans Luijten, and Nienke Bakker, eds., *Vincent van Gogh: The Letters* (Amsterdam and The Hague: Van Gogh Museum & Huygens ING, 2009), https://vangoghletters.org.

10. "Culture care" is to see culture as an ecosystem to steward, a garden to tend to, rather than a battleground to fight over. See my book *Culture Care: Reconnecting with Beauty for Our Common Life* (Downers Grove, IL: InterVarsity, 2014).

11. As I wrote this line, I had in front of me Anthony Doerr's remarkable book *All the Light We Cannot See* (New York: Scribner, 2017).

12. Many teachers have communicated this to me, including conductor Dr. David Gier.

13. See *Babette's Feast,* directed by Gabriel Axel, Nordisk Film, 1987, based upon the 1958 story by Isak Dinesen [Karen Blixen].

14. Such embedded thoughts are often exposed when artists come in to suggest creating something as a gratuitous offering. A typical response is, "Oh, that's nice but we don't have the budget for that" (as if artists paint only when there is "budget for the work"). Of course, such an act of generosity must be accompanied by proper curation. See "Mary's Response" in my book *Art and Faith: A Theology of Making* (New Haven: Yale University Press, 2021).

15. See Ken Sande, *The Peacemaker* (Ada, MI: Baker Books, 2004).

16. Rabbit skin glues, traditionally used for preparing Western canvases, are too strong and brittle for layering minerals on Japanese paper. Nikawa is designed for a multilayer process to build a durable surface without varnishing on paper or silk.

Chapter 2. Listening Room

1. Susan R. Barry, *Coming to Our Senses: A Boy Who Learned to See, a Girl Who Learned to Hear, and How We All Discover the World* (New York: Basic Books, 2021), 10.

2. I posit that in the process of making, we tap into the deeper connection between somatic knowledge and spiritual knowledge, or what the biblical writers call *epignosis.*

3. C. S. Lewis spoke of his imagination being baptized before he was (see

Lewis, *Surprised by Joy* [London: Geoffrey Bles, 1955]). Imagination, as Narnia's wardrobe door, is deeply connected with our faith through our senses. Imagination allows us to make sense of the myriads of information given to us every second and is a window into the rational order. Like Lewis, through my senses, my imagination was being baptized before my rational thoughts were.

4. William Blake, "The Everlasting Gospel," 1818, from *The Complete Writings of William Blake*, ed. Geoffrey Keynes (Oxford: Oxford University Press, 1972), plates 52–54, lines 99–102, 753.

5. Such a discovery of a deeper realm of "seeing" came through my faith journey. See "Behind the Veil," in the present book.

6. See these paintings and others referenced throughout on my website, https://makotofujimura.com.

7. I pursue a more tangible extension of my art into social practice at the end of this book.

8. See Madeleine L'Engle, *Walking on Water: Reflections on Faith and Art* (Wheaton, IL: Harold Shaw, 1980).

9. Saint Paul stated that in Christ, we are a new creation (2 Cor 5:17). The Greek word used for "new" is *kainos*, which means perpetually new and is a word I translate as "New Newness." This type of newness in Christ's resurrection defies our previous concept of what is new. Thus, it is not just a caterpillar becoming a butterfly, but it is an entirely new species, or even a new idea of a species of being. Enduring art will always enlighten the sense toward that deeper Reality behind our realities.

10. See Makoto Fujimura, "Jesus Is the God of Ground Zero," *Christianity Today*, Wondrous Cross issue (2022), https://www.christianitytoday.com/2022/02/lux-aeterna-god-ground-zero-makoto-fujimura/.

11. Morten Lauridsen, *Lux Aeterna*, LA Phil, accessed September 3, 2024, https://www.laphil.com/musicdb/pieces/5450/lux-aeterna.

12. See Makoto Fujimura, *Silence and Beauty: Hidden Faith Born of Suffering* (Downers Grove, IL: InterVarsity, 2017).

13. What would become bloody nationalism in the twentieth century was already present in the dictatorial forces of sixteenth-century consolidation and violence as the only means to advance power. Even today, Japan is assumed to be an island. But visually it is clear that Japan is really a peninsula connected to Korea and Russia. The dictatorial and nationalistic forces created a psycho-

logical barrier of isolationism and a false idol of power. Rikyū, by intentionally using Korean bowls to serve warlords about to invade Korea, or by using vessels often thought of as marginal, pushed back into power, creating room to consider peace. See Fujimura, *Silence and Beauty*.

Chapter 3. Sen no Rikyū

1. The pulverized form of green tea that was easy to transport started in the twelfth century; see Leo Kwan, "A (Very) Brief History of Green Tea," Tea Guardian, accessed September 3, 2024, https://www.teaguardian.com/what -is-tea/green-tea-history/.

2. See Makoto Fujimura, *Silence and Beauty: Hidden Faith Born of Suffering* (Downers Grove, IL: InterVarsity, 2017).

3. The founding of the *mingei* (Japanese folk art) movement led by Muneyoshi Yanagi developed this Korean influence further.

4. A third term, *suki*, is rarely discussed in the Western understanding of Rikyū's aesthetics. Suki literally means "to like," and connected sado words attach certain objects, such as *suki dogu*, which means "fine (or favorite) utensils." Suki also has an erotic undercurrent, a beauty of extravagance.

5. We have come to appreciate today, perhaps through social media, Japanese terms such as *shinrinryoku* (literally "bathing in forest" to seek inner calm in nature) or *shikataganai* ("there is nothing I can do" to understand the inevitability of decay and death). These words and values flow out of Rikyū's way of tea, but the Japanese may not be as keen to see these terms as important, as we in the West have found them to be.

6. See Beatrice M. Bodart, "Tea and Counsel: The Political Role of Sen Rikyū," *Monumenta Nipponica* 32, no. 1 (1977): 49–74, https://www.jstor.org/ stable/2384071.

7. What I have called their "*fumi-e* culture" is a portal into what I call "New Newness," which reshapes aesthetic history for generations to come. See Fujimura, *Silence and Beauty*, and Fujimura, *Art and Faith: A Theology of Making* (New Haven: Yale University Press, 2021).

8. See Fujimura, *Silence and Beauty*.

9. J. R. R. Tolkien and C. S. Lewis both experienced World War I as soldiers, and it is well-documented that out of their trauma came the characters and language of their stories, as well as their common bond of friendship at Oxford.

To survive the foxholes and dark trenches, including the horrific Battle of the Somme, Tolkien, surrounded by his dying friends, saw in his imagination a journey of the faithful soldiers willing to lay down their lives for "the war to end all wars." He began to name, one by one, characters and places of imagined reality based on these actual experiences in the trenches, which would later form the basis for *The Lord of the Rings*. Lewis, injured during the war, would create a story of the Pevensie children escaping London bombings through the wardrobe to Narnia. Their trauma and brokenness were a fissure that pushed them toward sanctified imagination, creating and making with golden words in spite of the Ground Zero ashes in front of them.

Similarly, T. S. Eliot's wartime journey to write *The Waste Land* came out of his trauma during the London bombings. In his *Four Quartets*, he prophetically describes "the unimaginable Zero summer" ("Little Gidding") of the atomic devastation before Hiroshima and Nagasaki (unintentionally), but the poem weaves in hope in the "still point of the turning world," capturing his own journey toward the light. These trauma experiences can connect the past and the present through art.

10. See Colossians 1. "You need to invite Christ into your heart (not just for salvation), but as your Creator," Tim Keller, conversation with the author.

11. To extend this thought further, what if our brokenness, through Christ's wounds, is healed not to the original perfection but to glorious imperfection? It is one thing to find glory in Christ's wounds, but what about in our wounds?

12. See Makoto Fujimura, *Culture Care: Reconnecting with Beauty for Our Common Life* (Downers Grove, IL: IVPress, 2014).

13. This statement was made at the Alliance for Responsible Citizenship conference, London, November 2023. See Alliance for Responsible Citizenship, "Are We Free When We Forget Ourselves | Joshua Luke Smith," YouTube video, November 13, 2023, https://www.youtube.com/watch?v=VjWxkUEJkqs.

Chapter 4. Art as Play

1. *Furoshiki* is used to wrap items to carry, but often it is used as a headdress or covering.

2. I learned later that it is due to "piloerection," a reflex caused by the activation of the sympathetic nervous system.

3. What if the Creator God desires to play with God's children, created in

God's image? What if art is a path to inner light that only our flights of imagination can lead us to?

4. For us to become children of God, as God calls us to be, we must develop a healthy interdependence and create culture care communities (see Behind the Veil: Section 2), where even adults can play.

5. Lilias Trotter, *Parables of the Cross* (London: Marshall Brothers, 1895), quoted in Clare Coffey, "Dandelions: An Apology," *Plough Quarterly* 39 (2024), published online March 19, 2024, https://www.plough.com/en/topics/justice/environment/dandelions-an-apology.

6. Jesus's gentle command in Matthew 6 to consider the lilies applies here because the "lilies" he spoke of are weedlike morning flowers that wilt by noon in the dry Galilean hills.

7. Haejin often comes in unannounced. Part of our relationship has been based on a unique trust. I had a vision when we were praying together while we were dating. I was inside my own painting: it was my own "interior castle," with a room full of azurite and lapis splendor. I then realized that someone else was in the room ahead of me. It was Haejin. It was the first time that I felt someone else's presence in this highly guarded space. To this day, she is the only person who can enter without my even knowing that she is there. She watches me paint, and documents that with photos and videos.

8. See Fujimura Listening Room (@fujimuralisteningroom) on Instagram.

9. Recently, during Holy Week, I watched rather mesmerized as we journeyed through Maundy Thursday, Good Friday, Holy Saturday, and Easter morning, sitting in front of the *Blueberry* painting each day. The smoky, refractive surface held the weight of the week, from Christ's washing of the disciples' feet, to his death on the cross, to the dark silence of waiting and then the glory of Easter morning. The unique quality of azurite is like a mirror, reflecting the meaning of each day; but also the color seemed to change with each morning light, sometimes reddish, sometimes cool blue, and in bright light, a refractive splendor.

Chapter 5. Slow Art

1. See my discussion of the Old English term *mearcstapa* (an Old English word for "border-stalker"), in Chapter 7 of *Culture Care: Reconnecting with Beauty for Our Common Life* (Downers Grove, IL: IVPress, 2014).

2. Jordan Kassalow, email correspondence with the author.

3. David Brooks, "Longing for an Internet Cleanse: A Small Rebellion Against the Quickening of Time," *New York Times,* March 28, 2019, https://www.nytimes.com/2019/03/28/opinion/internet-cleanse.html.

4. Makoto Fujimura, "The Aroma of the New" (2011 Belhaven University Commencement Address), June 15, 2021, https://makotofujimura.com/writings/the-aroma-of-the-new-2011-belhaven-university-commencement-address.

5. Western-style oil painting was called *yoga.* Some accounts state that Fenollosa himself invented the word "Nihonga," but recent conversations with curators and historians make me believe that it was the translator who created (perhaps with Fenollosa's knowledge) a word for "Japanese painting."

6. As I developed my art when I was an undergraduate student, it became clear that I needed to reexamine my own roots. That pilgrimage led me to Boston, my birthplace, and the seventeenth-century Japanese works in the Boston Museum of Fine Arts. What I saw there deeply moved me and eventually led to my applying, as a US citizen, for a governmental scholarship to return to Japan as a National Scholar.

7. I have noted in *Silence and Beauty* about how Japan is not an isolated island but a series of archipelagoes that connect South Korea and Russia. In an upside-down map of the geographical area, the Sea of Japan looks like a lake surrounded by a series of small, spotted islands.

8. For more on "common curse" and "common grace," see my 2023 Kuyper Award acceptance speech on my website under "Writings": "Kintsugi Grace—Prismatic Art Beyond the Rainbow," https://makotofujimura.com/writings/kintsugi-grace-prismatic-art-beyond-the-rainbow.

Chapter 6. Pulverized Minerals

1. Simone Weil, *Gravity and Grace,* trans. Emma Crawford and Mario von der Ruhr (London: Routledge, 2004), 5.

2. See Makoto Fujimura, "Fallen Towers and the Art of Tea," in *Refractions: A Journey of Faith, Art, and Culture* (Colorado Springs: NavPress, 2024).

3. See "Rothko: Pictures Must Be Miraculous," *American Masters,* season 22, episode 11, directed by Eric Slade, Public Broadcasting Corporation, aired October 25, 2019, https://www.pbs.org/wnet/americanmasters/rothko-pictures-must-be-miraculous-full-film/12085/.

4. See Makoto Fujimura, *Art and Faith: A Theology of Making* (New Haven: Yale University Press, 2021), 125.

5. My mentor Tim Keller defined, both in private conversations and in public speaking, an "idol" as "a good thing that we make ultimate. We say, 'Unless I have that, I am nothing.'"

6. Elaine Scarry, *On Beauty and Being Just* (Princeton, NJ: Princeton University Press, 2001), 31. Art finds her "shape of content" within the inherent confines of the medium itself—the boundaries, the "rules," emerge organically from the materials' limitations. Years of mastering the discipline of communication can also expose the idols lurking within, revealing and describing the shadows beneath the masks we wear. Art creates an arc toward the impossible, and anything, whether Moses's bronze serpent or a hero's statue, can become an idol. An idol's power resides not in the object, but in our hearts. As I have written in *Art and Faith,* faith is hard work (*ergon*) allowed by grace (*charis*) (Eph 2:8–10), and because it is a journey of discipline and love, any art can be liberated toward the presence of joy.

7. It took twenty years for me to recognize what my body already knew deeply in my bones—that I was suffering from undiagnosed post-traumatic stress disorder. I've experienced moments of what my therapist calls "deregulation"—when I feel my spirit leave my body, and at the same time, my body constricts helplessly as if I were trapped again in the No. 3 train, trying to get back home.

8. In the Bible, Daniel's friends Shadrach, Meshach, and Abednego refused to bow down to the gold statues set up to pay allegiance to King Nebuchadnezzar (Daniel 3) and saw an angel or "a son of the gods" walking with them into the furnace. Paul speaks of the sanctifying fire of judgment in 1 Corinthians 3. See Fujimura, *Art and Faith,* 77.

9. See Fujimura, "Fallen Towers."

Chapter 8. Soliloquies

1. As I have noted in other writings, I am grateful that some of the best Rouault paintings, especially from his *Passion* series, are collected in Japan. These paintings paved the way for my faith.

2. The exhibit was organized by the Rouault Estate and Dillon Gallery, 2009.

3. From the original manuscript for Thomas Hibbs, *Soliloquies* (Baltimore: Square Halo Books, 2009).

4. See more on ecosystems of culture in my lecture "Emily Dickinson, Rachel Carson and the New Creation," October 28, 2018, https://makoto fujimura.com/writings/emily-dickinson-rachel-carson-and-the-new-creation.

5. Second Corinthians 12:7: "So to keep me from becoming conceited because of the surpassing greatness of the revelations, a thorn was given me in the flesh" (ESV).

6. See Makoto Fujimura, "Fra Angelico and the Five-Hundred-Year Question," in *Refractions: A Journey of Faith, Art, and Culture* (Colorado Springs: Nav-Press, 2024).

7. See David Kelsey, *Eccentric Existence: A Theological Anthropology* (Louisville: Westminster John Knox, 2009).

8. Mark Rothko, *Mark Rothko: A Consummated Experience Between Picture and Onlooker* (Riehen, Basel: Fondation Beyeler, 2001), 22.

9. Haejin and I continued to exchange the panels for each liturgical season during the COVID-19 pandemic, even though no one could see them in person.

Chapter 9. Interdependence of Colors

1. Jesus announced, "I am the light of the world" (John 8:12). Saint Augustine took this passage quite literally. As Jesus is also the Creator (Colossians 1), we can say that he is the uncreated reality of light itself. It would make sense, from this perspective, that whether we believe this claim of Jesus or not, he held multiple paradoxes together in his very historical presence. Jesus promises, in that sense, to shed holy light onto the fragmented reality in front of us.

2. See "Behind the Veil" below for my meditation on Tabasco sauce branding design, a simple but brilliant use of complementary colors.

3. Even those who intentionally isolate themselves often do so in community, such as in a monastery. Similarly, hermetic literature such as Henry David Thoreau's *Walden* was written precisely to *communicate* his solitary journey to readers.

4. See Emily Dickinson's untitled poem #1463 (c. 1879), published as "A route of evanescence" in *The Complete Poems of Emily Dickenson* (Boston: Little, Brown, 1924), 86.

5. See Makoto Fujimura, "Fra Angelico and the Five-Hundred-Year Ques-

tion," in *Refractions: A Journey of Faith, Art, and Culture* (Colorado Springs: NavPress, 2024). Also published online at https://makotofujimura.com under "Writings."

6. When I read passages from the book of Revelation about the New Jerusalem, the descriptions seem close to that reality of prismatic refractions and pure gold (which is liquid) as we walk on golden waters and witness the golden city of New Jerusalem descending into the New Earth. Perhaps in the surface portal of painting, we can see what that experience will be like, thus preparing us for the feast on the other side of eternity even as we labor on this side of scarcity.

Chapter 10. Jacob's Ladder

1. I am grateful for the Windrider Studios team (see the Windrider Institute at https://www.windriderinstitute.org).

Chapter 11. A Magnificent Longing

1. The Fujimura Fellows program ran from 2015 to 2025 under the Fujimura Institute in collaboration with Fuller Theological Seminary's Brehm Center and Bucknell University.

2. September G. Penn, "Through His Brokenness," July 7, 2020, https://septemberpenn.bandcamp.com/track/through-his-brokenness. Thanks to September G. and Ivan Penn, cofounders of "The Power of Song," for granting permission to retell this story and print the song lyrics here.

3. See Makoto Fujimura, *Culture Care: Reconnecting with Beauty for Our Common Life* (Downers Grove, IL: IVPress, 2014), 66–68.

4. Windrider Studios recorded the live painting and tea ceremony: Makoto Fujimura, "New Wine Full Performance," YouTube Video, 10:07, May 29, 2018, https://youtu.be/2ZGhxCzYlEw?si=e-GLioUgfQjUMwvd.

5. No one wins culture wars. If we "win," we do so by demonizing and scapegoating "the other," and in doing so we poison the very soil of the culture we are trying to cultivate for the next generation. Culture care is needed, first for the mending of the decimated lands of culture wars, but also for creation care. Without the language to mediate the polarization, any effort to speak of the environment will be hijacked by culture war language and rhetoric.

6. Artists, too, are the "canary in the coal mine" of culture. We detect such poisonous air and sing.

7. I am grateful for my conversation with the late Dr. Tim Keller at the exhibit of *Nagasaki Koi*, whose words at the time have continued to influence my thoughts on this. See also my recent lecture at the University of Pennsylvania as an EAVS (Equity in Action Visiting Scholars) fellow: https://makoto fujimura.com/writings/postdestruction.

8. Many years ago, Nigel Goodwin, a mentor to many artists of faith in the United Kingdom, said to me, "We are not human doings, but human beings, and human becomings." In the studio is where my "doing" becomes part of my "being" and "becoming" through the unraveling rhythm of my poem/*poiema* (the Greek word for "that which has been made or done," from which we get the word "poem") of my own journey. I posit these words as a guidepost for future generations to discover and perhaps find refuge in.

Definitions

1. My effort on social media using the hashtags #SunriseIsSunset or #SunsetIsSunrise puts this notion in action, to be aware of the common experience of both beauty and suffering. A sunrise is a sunset elsewhere. For more on "common curse," see a talk I gave in 2023 when I received the Kuyper Prize: "Kintsugi Grace—Prismatic Art Beyond the Rainbow," https://makotofujimura. com/writings/kintsugi-grace-prismatic-art-beyond-the-rainbow.

2. See Makoto Fujimura, *Silence and Beauty: Hidden Faith Born of Suffering* (Downers Grove, IL: InterVarsity, 2017).

Behind the Veil

1. William Blake, *Jerusalem,* ed. E. R. D. Maclagan and A. G. B. Russell (London: A. H. Bullen, 1904), plate 96, lines 8–28; see also https://commons.wiki media.org/wiki/Category:Jerusalem_The_Emanation_of_the_Giant_Albion.

2. See Ken Sande, *The Peacemaker* (Ada, MI: Baker Books, 2004).

Acknowledgments

Coram Deo

I am eternally grateful for my bride, Haejin, who daily reminds me of what it means to live out *Coram Deo*. Her law firm Shim & Associates represents me as my "general counsel," and their advocacy has empowered all I do as an artist. I am also grateful for our creative officer, Jacob Beaird, who has done an invaluable job in keeping this project aligned and managing the details toward completion.

Thanks also to my editor at Yale University Press, Jennifer Banks, for desiring to create a "beautiful book" coming out of our pandemic malaise, and for guiding me to focus on what I see.

This book is dedicated to the memory of my mother, who saw something in her three-year-old that made her keep that first painting, and of my father, a scientist who wanted to be an artist.

Index